The Romance of the
Patchwork Quilt in America

The Romance of the
Patchwork Quilt
In America

IN THREE PARTS

PART I
History and Quilt Patches

PART II
Quilts—Antique and Modern

BY CARRIE A. HALL

PART III
Quilting and Quilting Designs

BY ROSE G. KRETSINGER

PHOTOGRAPHS BY MARY ELLEN EVERHARD

BONANZA BOOKS • NEW YORK

This edition published by Bonanza Books,
a division of Crown Publishers, Inc.

Printed in the United States of America

TO

QUILT LOVERS—EVERYWHERE

World Without End

FOREWORD

THIS book is a human record of a homecraft art that has played no small part in the growth and development of American life across the ages from the earliest Colonial times to the present day. First as a necessary part of pioneer home-making, then as a product of an awakened desire for beauty in the home, and now this twentieth century revival is an appreciation of that art, which of all the time-honored household arts has withstood the machine age, and has by no means reached its climax.

When the World War was over and there was no longer a necessity for knitting socks and sweaters, I found my fingers itching for some "pick-up" work, so I turned to quilt-making, which had always interested me from the time when on my seventh birthday my pioneer mother cut the patches for a star quilt that under her watchful guidance proved a masterpiece that was a nine-day wonder in the neighborhood.

Quilt-making proved to be very interesting "pick-up" work. In fact, it not only kept my fingers busy, but it stimulated my imagination and I created several new designs. After completing my "baker's dozen" I realized that I couldn't continue making quilts indefinitely, and yet I was so fascinated by all the numerous and beautiful patterns that I conceived the idea of making a collection of patches, one like every known pattern, little realizing the magnitude of the undertaking. The collection now contains over one thousand patches and is to be placed in the Thayer Museum of Art of the University of Kansas.

Having displayed the collection on several occasions, I have been persuaded to put it into book form, so that my friends, and all others who love quilts and are actively engaged in quilting, may enjoy it. Some seven hundred of these patches are reproduced in this book, together with a short history of the origin and development of patchwork in America.

Patterns were collected from every available source and grateful acknowledgment is herewith made to:

All my friends, who so generously assisted in a still hunt for quilt patterns, old and new. Also to:

Old Patchwork Quilts and the Women Who Made Them, by Ruth Finley; *Quilts, Their Story and How to Make Them,* by Marie D. Webster; *Old Fashioned Quilts,* by Carlie Sexton; The Thayer Museum of Art; *The Kansas City Star; The Seattle Post-Intelligencer* and Prudence Penny; Grandmother Clark's Old Fashioned Quilt Designs; The McKim Studios; *The Woman's Home Companion; The Ladies' Home Journal; The Modern Priscilla; The Household Magazine; The Royal Neighbor;* The Ladies' Art Co.; Mountain Mist Quilting Cotton; and many from sources unknown.

In making this collection I found that nearly all of the better-known designs were included in every commercialized group offered for sale.

One of the most pleasing phases of this research work has been the discovery of many beautiful quilts, owned by friends which are reproduced in Part II.

CARRIE A. HALL

Maplehurst,
Leavenworth, Kansas
May 1933.

"Here practise and invention may be free
And as a squirrel skips from tree to tree,
So maids may (from their mistresse or their mother)
Learn to leave one worke, and learne another.
For here they may make choice of which is which,
And skip from worke to worke, from stitch to stitch,
Until, in time, delightful practise shall
(With profit) make them perfect in them all.
Thus hoping that these workes may have this guide
To serve for ornament, and not for pride:
To cherish verture, banish idlenesse,
For these ends, may this booke have good successe."

The Needle's Excellency—John Taylor, 1580-1653

Table of Contents

PART I

Origin and History of Quilt-making with Photographic Reproductions of Patches

PART II

Quilts of Colonial Ancestry and of Modern Design

PART III

The Art of Quilting and Quilting Designs

Part 1

Origin and History of Quilt-making With
Photographic Reproductions of
Patches

1

THE ROMANCE OF PATCHWORK

QUILT-MAKING is one of the most fascinating forms of needlecraft. It is occupying the attention of womankind everywhere, and every enthusiastic quilter who has one or more under construction is eagerly hunting for new patterns. These must be authentic antique designs or, if modern, have definite artistic merit.

Broadly speaking, anything made of two pieces of material with padding between and held together with stitches is a quilt. Common usage has restricted the term to bed-covering. A quilter is one who makes patchwork or applique work, or who quilts the top and lining together.

As known today, the quilt is the result of combining two kinds of needlework, both of very ancient origin but widely different in character. Patchwork is the art of piecing together fabrics of various kinds and colors; quilting is the method of fastening together layers of cloth to secure firmly the "filling," the amount of which is entirely governed by the need of protection against rigorous climates.

The quilt, as we know it in America, was in the beginning a strictly utilitarian article, born of the necessity of providing warm covers for beds and hangings for doors and windows that were not sufficiently fitted to keep out the cold of a New England winter, and were so intimately connected with the everyday life of the colonists that no record of them exists. What was yesterday a necessity is today a luxury.

We learn from Colonial history that there were three primary groups of colonists: the New Englanders with their abstract and positive theologies; the Dutch with their home-making instincts; and the luxury-loving Virginians.

The unrestraint of the civilization that the colonists had left behind them had made its mark upon their character. Within the four walls of the crude log cabins there was little thought of adornment or art, and yet the artistic longing, latent or inherent in every woman where her home is concerned, unconsciously expressed itself in her patchwork. The keener her sense of the artistic the more intricate her quilt patterns and the finer her stitches in the quilting of her masterpiece. Who shall say that woman's mind is inferior to man's, when, with no knowledge of mathematics, these women worked out geometric designs so intricate, and co-related each patch to all others in the block?

Needlework, like other phases of human endeavor, runs true to type, as is reflected in the quilt names and designs of each different locality. These designs were used again and again by succeeding generations, without any variations until after the Revolution, when families from each of these groups joined in the settlement of Kentucky, Ohio, Indiana, and other central states known to them as the "West." Women who in pioneering days unflinchingly turned their faces westward toward hardship and danger that the nation might expand were delighted with the opportunity thus afforded to exchange quilt patterns.

Every ambitious quilter with originality and artistic instincts delights in changing and improving designs; so these young pioneers, using the old patterns as a foundation, worked out new designs and christened them to suit their new environment. Hence, it is not unusual to find patterns of the same design having different names.

Under the general title of "Patchwork" we may consider three different kinds of quilts. First: the pieced quilt, showing the pieced patch set together in various ways and subsequently quilted in designs specially adapted to its requirements. Nearly all quilts made in America prior to 1750 were pieced quilts, and we love to think of some Dutch or New England housewife spreading the first pieced quilt over her frontier bed. Second: the appliqued, patched, or "laid-on" quilt, usually of floral design and considered more elegant than the humble "pieced" variety. Applique for quilt-making came into favor about the middle of the eighteenth century and reached its climax about 1850. With the revival of patchwork in the twentieth century it has reached a perfection of artistic color-combination and needlecraft far superior to anything made in earlier times. Third: the quilted counterpane—usually white, where decoration is obtained by means of padded or corded quilting in more or less elaborate design. Examples of these may be seen in PARTS II and III of this book.

The pieced quilt (made of pieces of fabric cut after patterns and sewed together to form a block or repeat) was familiar to most households where economy was a necessity, as it was created of scraps of material not otherwise of use. The pieced quilt in pioneer days provided means of turning to good account the precious scraps of printed cottons, at that period so rare and costly. The use of so many tiny pieces in one quilt and the pride with which the number—often in the thousands—was announced, gave evidence of their patience and frugality. One notable example had thirty thousand pieces, each of which measured just one fourth by three fourths of an inch in size. In these days of hurry and stress it is difficult to envision the woman with leisure and patience for such a task.

The appliqued quilt is apt to be a more artistic expression of the quilters craft, in that it is created "out of whole cloth," so to speak, and offers correspondingly greater freedom for the expression of the designer's artistic capabilities. In the old days, however, it was often combined with piecework, so that the gap in the family's comfort was bridged with both comeliness and efficacy.

In pattern and workmanship, the pieced quilt seems indigenous to American soil. Mrs. Wiggs, of Cabbage Patch fame, said piecing quilts was "keepin' the peace and doin' away with the scraps." The pieced quilt, though considered in the old days as inferior to the elaborately quilted or appliqued quilt, is today almost equally valued because of the excellence of some of the designs, and because of its association with the four-poster beds of olden times. Among fabrics that went into it were bits of dresses of the women members of the family and their friends. Sometimes such pieces were intentionally used to make a "keepsake" quilt, and for years pieces of grandmother's wedding dress would be pointed out to the grandchildren.

History tells us very little about the patchwork quilt prior to 1750, but in the one hundred years between 1750 and 1850 many quilts were pieced and patched and many of them are now the cherished possessions of great-granddaughters of the original makers. Time adds significance to *every* quilt, whether you make it yourself or receive it as a gift.

The art of quilt-making is still widely practiced in the southern mountains where life is still as simple and unhurried as it was a century ago. The mountain women still make their original patterns and have no conception of life as lived in a twentieth century city. The quilt as developed by mistresses of the great plantation homes of the south was quite a different product. Made of the finest fabrics and with a premeditated color scheme, it was the quintessence of refinement and taste.

Many of the eighteenth century quilts were square, as the beds of that period were wider than those of the present day. Many were made of four blocks measuring thirty-six inches square, to which was added an eighteen-inch border, making the finished quilt one hundred and eight inches square—almost large enough for the "Great Bed of Ware." Elaborate designs such as "Ben Hur's Chariot Wheel," the "Princess Feather," the "California Plume," or the "Rose of Sharon" were used for quilts of this type, and the border was designed to carry out the same motif or it might be a "Saw Tooth" pattern with no thought of the incongruity of the effect. Border effects were simple or elaborate according to the ambition of the maker. Many of these quilts were so elaborate that years were spent in the making and the quilting—no wonder they are cherished as precious heirlooms and occupy honored places in our homes and in our museums.

Even in Grandmother's day they were too fine for common use, being used only as counterpanes when very special guests were entertained, the circuit-riding minister or the presiding elder being the ones most often thus honored; and now they are brought out and displayed at the most pretentious "Quilt Shows" where countless throngs admire them and envy the fortunate owners. The appliqued quilt was considered more worthy of the place of honor in the home than the pieced quilt, unless it was a veritable masterpiece, and for this reason most of the antique quilts handed down to this generation are of the applique variety.

Anything so intimately bound up in the history of a country will reappear from time to time in popularity. The present revival began about 1915 but was submerged by knitting during the World War. Following the war the interest was renewed, and quilt-piecing in every home from Maine to California became one of the vital interests of the day. More quilts are being pieced today in the cities and on the farms than at any previous time in the history of America, and these new ones have the charm of Colonial design and meticulous handiwork. Manufacturers of cotton prints revived many of the early nineteenth century designs, to the delight of every quilter, and the quilts of this period will be treasured by daughters, granddaughters, and great-granddaughters yet unborn.

In the ready-cut quilts offered for sale are seen the effects of this hurrying age in which we live. This is especially distressing to the "true quilter" for, as Aunt Jane of Kentucky says: "There is a heap of comfort in making quilts, just to sit and sort over the pieces and call to mind that this piece or that is of the dress of a loved friend." How can the modern quilt-maker know any of that joy if she must go to the store and buy her patches, an eighth of a yard here and another there —or buy a ready-cut quilt?

2

QUILT NAMES

ALL the old favorite quilt patches had interesting generic names. These names are intriguing, and in nearly every instance there was a reason or at least a suggestion for the name, but many of these patches have been so changed that it requires a real stretch of the imagination to see any semblance of pattern to name. Religion, occupations, politics, nature in its various phases, and their meager social activities all contributed their quota to the quilt names of Colonial days.

The "Star" quilt in its numerous variations easily leads all the rest. Over one hundred different star patterns are shown in Part I of this book. Next in number and variety of design is the ever beautiful "Rose," the "Rose of Sharon" being the favorite. It seems to have had a special significance for brides. Fortunate was the bride whose dower-chest contained a "Rose of Sharon" quilt, and it was frequently saved for guests of honor and special occasions. These quilts last forever and ever and many a bride of today has tucked away in her "hope chest" the same beautiful quilt her grandmother made for her own "dower-chest."

A source of inspiration quite prolific was the trades and occupations of the times: "Anvil," "Saw-Tooth," "The Ship's Wheel," "Carpenter's Wheel," "Double Monkey Wrench," "Churn Dash," "Water Mill," "Chips and Whetstones," "The Reel," "The Dusty Miller," and many others. The mill and the miller was one of the familiar figures of Colonial days and, as water was the only power, they were located wherever there was a natural mill-site so the roads leading up and down the hills and valleys were the main-traveled roads.

From their flower gardens came all the wide range of flower names. Applique offers free scope for one's fancy or artistic feeling, having no set design, no actual pattern that one must follow; therefore, no two appliqued quilts are ever exactly alike, either in detail or coloring. All garden varieties of flowers are the usual motif for applique quilts. Many of the names were so much a part of their simple outdoor life that one can reconstruct much of it by a study of such names as: "Garden Maze," "Sun Dial," "Autumn Leaf," "Spider Web," "Rolling Stone," "Flying Bats," "Dove-in-the-Window," "Devil's Claws," and "Ocean Wave." "Brown Goose," or "Gray Goose," according to the predominating color of the patches, reminds one of the old lullaby, "The Old Gray Goose is Dead."

Quilt names were sometimes suggested by recreation but these were few in comparison with the names furnished by work and duty, showing that their lives were far more serious than frivolous; but the square dance was one of their pleasures and was the usual happy ending of the quilting bee. From it we get such names as "Eight Hands Around," "Swing-in-the-Center," and others.

There were scores of political names given to their quilts by those who were conscious of the great change brought about by the Revolution and their new freedom. Not having a vote, they did not talk politics as do the women of this twentieth century, but they listened to the discussions of the men and formed opinions and were true to their own convictions of party loyalty. Such names as "Clay's Choice," "Whig Rose," "Democrat Rose," "Harrison Rose," "Fifty-Four-Forty-or-Fight," "The Little Giant," "Lincoln's Platform," "Old Tippecanoe," and "Free Trade Patch" are of political inspiration.

Many quilt names are common only to the community in which they originated; thus a patch known as "Rock Glen" in the mountains of Kentucky and Tennessee is called "Lost Ship" by those living near the seacoast. Most of the names have been multiplied by changing conditions and migrations and by variation of the quilter's whim, facetious or sincere, until the original name is lost. And it is a fact to be deplored that, for commercial purposes, the old time patterns are being offered for sale under newly-coined names, thus destroying all the romance attached to the names familiar in Colonial and Pioneer days.

There were numerous names having the "Sun" as the inspiration motif: "Rising Sun," "Setting Sun," "Sunburst," "Sunbeam"; also "Indian Summer" and all the numerous family of "Sunflower" patches. The "Rising Sun" is the acme of perfection in pieced patchwork. Last, but by no means least, are all the numerous patches having Bible names. Their religion was such a vital part of the lives of our ancestors that it is not strange that there were many of these. "Job's Tears," "Joseph's Coat," "Jacob's Ladder," "Crown of Thorns," "Wonder-of-the-World," "Ecclesiastes," "Children of Israel," "Golgotha," "David and Goliath," "Coronation," and innumerable ones having "Cross" as an integral part. "Crosses and Losses" belongs to this group. These names are as full of imagination as the quilts were of color, and the girl of today following the patterns originated by her great-grandmother when she was young, may boast that her gorgeously colored *new* quilt looks futuristic, with its cubistic pattern of small triangles one way, crossing large triangles the other, into a gay syncopation of stuttering angles and planes.

One of the very interesting old quilts having scriptural significance was called a "Scripture Quilt," each block having a large white square in the center on which a scripture quotation or an old adage of high moral tendency was embroidered in turkey red cotton (because it was fast color and wouldn't *run* when washed). I remember one in our home on which this verse was embroidered: "Learn to be useful and not fanciful. From your Aunt Sally, 1848." Then there was the "Bride's Quilt," each block made by a friend, inscribed with her name and presented to the bride; and the "Album" quilt, each block made by a member of the congregation with her name embroidered on it, which when set together and quilted by the Ladies' Aid Society was presented to the minister's wife.

In this book you will find the pictured patches grouped according to their own classification and many names in addition to those included in this list.

3

THE QUILTING BEE

SOCIAL life in pioneer days was necessarily very limited. Not having the modern conveniences for exchanging choice bits of gossip, the quilting bee afforded an excellent means of "broadcasting" the latest events, such as Mary's engagement or the arrival of Susie's new baby girl, as well as the state of the spring and fall housecleaning.

During the close confinement of the long winter days the women-folk of the family spent their spare time piecing and patching quilt tops to replenish the family supply—and many lovely ones to tuck away in daughter's dower-chest. There were no central heating plants such as we know today, and in very early Colonial days no heating stoves, only fireplaces and those usually confined to the kitchen and general living room, the parlor, with drawn blinds, being used only for very special company, weddings, and funerals; so there was no room in which to "put up" a quilt for quilting during the winter months.

With the coming of spring the various blocks were "set together" and sometimes a border was added, especially if the quilt was considered extra choice or was intended for the dower-chest; then it was ready for the quilting. Invitations were sent to the nearest neighbors, and joyful preparations made for a real social function, second in importance only to the meetings of religious nature.

Having breakfasted at five or six o'clock, the quilters arrived early on the gala day and began work at once, marking the design with chalk, using a dinner plate for the center of the feather wreath design, and many other devices known only to those to whom "necessity is the mother of invention." The social, gossipy interchange of neighborhood news did not interrupt the swiftly flying fingers of those expert quilters, but seemed rather to add to their agility.

The housewife-hostess had ample opportunity to display her culinary accomplishments, for the meals to be served received as much careful attention as do the bridge luncheons of the present day. At eleven o'clock the workers were called to dinner which consisted of all the delicacies the cellar and larder afforded. Recipes for all sorts of pickles, preserves, and cake were discussed and exchanged. Then back to the quilt which must be finished before five, for late in the afternoon the men-folk of the various families—husbands, brothers, and sweethearts—came to share in the *supper* which was served between five and six o'clock. This meal was often more elaborate than the one served at noonday, for does not the old adage say "The way to a man's heart is through his stomach"?

The men compared notes on the latest planting and other neighborhood affairs while the younger members of the families played games; the arrival of the fiddlers heralded the beginning of a very joyous occasion—the country dance—and everyone, old and young, entered into the spirit of the dance which was the end of a perfect day. It is from this that we get such quilt names as "Hands-all-Around," and "Swing-in-the-Center." As folk-songs, "Yankee Doodle" and "Dixie" are no more characteristically American than is "Aunt Dinah's Quilting Party," written by Stephen C. Foster in 1850.

One custom that was common in every locality was the making of "Album" quilts. They were highly prized, and especially so when they were made by the women of the congregation as a gift to the minister's wife. Each woman made a block with her name embroidered in the center, then they were set together and a grand "quilting bee" was given at the home of the minister if he had a local church and lived among his flock, but if he was a "circuit rider" and served many communities the quilting was at the home of one of the members of the congregation. It was much the same as other quiltings except that the conversation was apt to take a more religious turn and "old and new doctrine," "original sin," and unregenerate doings were frequently discussed, especially after the arrival of the men-folk for supper which was the fitting finale of such an occasion.

Susan B. Anthony, the great "Woman Statesman," who gave half a century of service to help the women of America, delivered her first talk in the cause of "Equal Rights" at a meeting of this kind.

The description of the quilting bee in Mrs. Harriet Beecher Stowe's book, "The Minister's Wooing," is rich in New England lore. An excerpt follows:

The rattling of wheels was heard at the gate, and Candace, Mrs. Marvin's cook, was discerned, seated aloft in the one-horse wagon, with her usual complement of baskets and bags.

"Well, now, dear me! if there isn't Candace!" said Miss Prissy; "I do believe Miss Marvin has sent her with something for the quilting!" and out she flew as nimble as a humming bird, while those in the house heard various exclamations of admiration, as Candace, with stately dignity, disinterred from the wagon one basket after another, and exhibited to Miss Prissy's enraptured eyes sly peeps under the white napkins with which they were covered. And then, hanging a large basket on either arm, she rolled majestically towards the house, like a heavy-laden India-man coming in after a fast voyage.

"Good-mornin', Miss Scudder! Good-mornin', Doctor!" she said, dropping her curtsey on the doorstep; "Good-mornin', Miss Mary! Ye see our folks was stirrin' pooty early dis mornin' an' Miss Marvin sent me down wid two or tree little tings."

Setting her baskets on the floor, and seating herself between them, she proceeded to develop their contents with ill-concealed triumph. One basket was devoted to cakes of every species, from the great Mont-Blanc loaf-cake, with its snowy glaciers of frosting, to the twisted cruller and puffy doughnut. In the other basket lay pats of golden butter curiously stamped, reposing on a bed of fresh green leaves, while currants, red and white, and delicious cherries and raspberries, gave a final finish to the picture. From a basket which Miss Prissy brought in from the rear appeared cold fowl and tongue delicately prepared, and shaded with feathers of parsley. Candace, whose rolicking delight in the good things of this life was conspicuous in every emotion, might have furnished to a painter, as she sat in her brilliant turban, an idea for an African Genius of Plenty.

"Why, really, Candace," said Mrs. Scudder, "you are overwhelming us!"

"Ho! Ho! Ho!" said Candace, "I's tellin' Miss Marvin folks don't git married but once in der lives, (gin'ally speakin', dat is) an' den dey oughter hab plenty to do it wid."

"Well, I must say," said Miss Prissy, taking out the loaf-cake with busy assiduity, "I must say, Candace, this does beat all!"

"I should rader tink it oughter," said Candace, bridling herself with proud consciousness; "ef it don't, 'taint 'cause ole Candace hain't put enough into it. I tell ye, I didn't do nothin' all day yisterday but jes' make dat ar cake. Cato, when he got up, he begun to talk some-h'n 'bout his shirt buttons, an' I jes' shet him right up. I says, 'Cato, when I's r'ally got a cake to make for a great 'casion, I wants my mind *jest* as quiet an' *jest* as serene as ef I was agoin' to de sacrament. I don't want no 'arthly cares on it. Now,' says I, 'Cato, de ole Doctor's gwine to be married, and dis yer's his quiltin' cake; an' Miss Mary, she's gwine to be married, an' dis yer's *her* quiltin' cake. An' dar'll be eberybody to dat ar quiltin', an' ef de cake ain't right, why, 't would be puttin' a candle under a bushel. An' so,' says I, 'Cato, your buttons must wait.' An' Cato, he sees de 'priety ob it, 'cause, dough he can't make cake like me, he's a 'mazin' good judge on't, an' is dreful tickled when I slips out a little loaf for his supper."

"How is Mrs. Marvin?" said Mrs. Scudder.

"Kinder thin and shimmery; but she's about,—habin' her eyes ebery-war 'n' lookin' into eberyting. She jes' touches tings wid de tips ob her fingers an' dey seem to go like. She'll be down to de quiltin' dis arter-noon. But she tole me to take de tings an' come down an' spend de day here; for Miss Marvin an' I both knows how many steps mus' be taken sech times, an' we agreed you oughter favor yourselves all you could."

"Well, now," said Miss Prissy, lifting up her hands, "if that ain't what 't is to have friends! Why, that was one of the things I was thinking of, as I lay awake last night; because, you know, at times like these, people run their feet off before the time begins, and then they are all limpsey and lop-sided when the time comes. Now, I say, Candace, all Miss Scudder and Mary have to do is to give everything up to us, and we'll put it through straight."

"Dat's what we will!" said Candace. "Jes' show me what's to be done, an' I'll do it."

Candace and Miss Prissy soon disappeared together into the pantry with the baskets, whose contents they began busily to arrange. Candace shut the door, that no sound might escape, and began a confidential out-pouring to Miss Prissy.

"Ye see," she said, "I'se *feelin's* all de while for Miss Marvin; 'cause, ye see, she was expectin', ef eber Mary was married—well—dat 'twould be to somebody else, ye know—our Mass'r Jim."

By two o'clock a goodly company began to assemble. Mrs. Deacon Twitchell arrived, soft, pillowy, and plaintive as ever, accompanied by Cerinthy Ann, a comely damsel, tall and trim, with a bright black eye and a most vigorous and determined style of movement. Good Mrs. Jones, broad, expansive, and solid, having vegetated tranquilly on in the cabbage garden of the virtues since three years ago when she graced our tea party, was now as well preserved as ever, and brought some fresh butter, a tin pail of cream, and a loaf of cake made after a new Philadelphia receipt.

The quilt-pattern was gloriously drawn in oak leaves, done in indigo; and soon all the company, young and old, were passing busy fingers over it, and conversation went on briskly.

Madam de Frontignac, we must not forget to say, had entered with hearty *abandon* into the spirit of the day; she would have her seat and soon won the respect of the party by the dexterity with which she used her needle; though, when it was whispered that she learned to quilt among the nuns, some of the elderly ladies exhibited a slight uneasiness, as being rather doubtful whether they might not be encouraging papistical opinions by allowing her an equal share in the work of getting up their minister's bed-quilt; but the younger part of the company were quite captivated by her foreign air, and the pretty manner in which she lisped her English; and Cerinthy Ann even went so far as to horrify her mother by saying that she wished she'd been educated in a convent herself,—a declaration which arose less from native depravity than from a certain vigorous disposition, which often shows itself in young people, to shock the current opinions of their elders and betters. Of course, the conversation took a general turn, somewhat in unison with the spirit of the occasion; and whenever it flagged, some allusion to a forthcoming wedding, or some sly hint as the future young Madame of the parish, was sufficient to awaken the dormant animation of the company.

Cerinthy Ann contrived to produce an agreeable electric shock by declaring that for her part she never could see into it, how any girl could marry a minister; that she should as soon think of setting up housekeeping in a meeting house.

"Oh, Cerinthy Ann!" exclaimed her mother, "how can you go on so?"

"It's a fact," said the adventurous damsel; "now other men let you have some peace, but a minister's always around under your feet."

"So you think the less you see of a husband, the better?" said one of the ladies.

"Just my views," said Cerinthy Ann, giving a decided snip to her thread with her scissors. "I like the Nantucketers, that go off on four-years' voyages and leave their wives a clear field. If I ever get married, I'm going up to have one of those fellows."

"You'd better take care, Cerinthy Ann," said her mother. "They say that 'those who sing before breakfast will cry before supper.' Girls talk about getting married," she said, relapsing into a gentle didactic melancholy, "without realizing its awful responsibilities."

"Oh, as to that," said Cerinthy, "I've been practising on my pudding now these six years, and I shouldn't be afraid to throw one up a chimney with any girl."

This speech was founded on a tradition, current in those times, that no young lady was fit to be married till she could construct a boiled

Indian pudding of such consistency that it could be thrown up a chimney and come down on the ground outside without breaking; and the consequences of Cerinthy Ann's sally was a general laugh.

"Girls ain't what they used to be in my day," sententiously remarked an elderly lady. "I remember my mother told me when she was thirteen she could knit a long cotton stocking in a day."

"I haven't much faith in these stories of old times—have you, girls?" said Cerinthy, appealing to the younger members at the frame.

"At any rate," said Mrs. Twitchel, "our minister's wife will be a pattern; I don't know anybody that goes beyond her either in spinning or fine stitching."

Thus the day was spent in friendly gossip as they quilted and rolled and talked and laughed, and as the afternoon sun cast lengthening shadows on the grass Mary and Miss Marvin went into the great kitchen, where a long table stood exhibiting all that plentitude of provision which the immortal description of Washington Irving has saved us the trouble of recapitulating in detail.

The husbands, brothers, and lovers had come in, and the scene was redolent of gayety. When Mary made her appearance, there was a moment's pause, till she was conducted to the side of the Doctor; when, raising his hand, he invoked a grace upon the loaded board.

Unrestrained gayeties followed. Groups of young men and maidens chatted together, and all the gallantries of the times were enacted. Serious matrons commented on the cake, and told each other high and particular secrets in the culinary art, which they drew from remote family archives. One might have learned in that instructive assembly how best to keep moths out of blankets; how to make fritters of Indian corn undistinguishable from oysters; how to bring up babies by hand; how to mend a cracked teapot; how to take out grease from a brocade; how to reconcile absolute decrees with free will; how to make five yards of cloth answer the purpose of six; and how to put down the Democratic party. All were busy, earnest, and certain, just as a swarm of men and women, old and young, are in 1859.

The Bureau of Rural Life of the National Congress of Parents and Teachers in an annual convention recently held in Denver, urged a return of the "quilting party" from which the young man of yesteryear used to see "Nellie" home, as a curb on modern youth.

4

THE QUILT'S PLACE IN ART

THE making of patchwork quilts is one of the most picturesque of all the folk-arts. It is the only one of the home-craft arts that has withstood the machine age. The beauty which has its expression in the work of our architects, artists, and poets of today oftentimes had its first fling in these humble creations in the hands of our pioneer mothers. Needlework was the one art which women could claim as their own. In every household, rich or poor, women sewed; the rich had their silks and embroideries; the poor the more practical art of making their own clothes and household supplies. Teaching the young girls to sew was the first thing they did, and teaching embroidery stitches for pay might be termed the first business in which women engaged. Even those who had means must think of necessities, and in a large family the ever increasing demand for bed-quilts, so essential to their comfort, made them the universal form of needlework prior to 1750. In mansion house or frontier cabin, every scrap was saved for the quilt making.

Alice Morse Earl, in *Home Life in Colonial Days*, writes of the fondness for patchwork of our great-grandmothers, and how highly they prized bits of highly colored fabrics. She says:

The feminine love of color, the longing for decoration, as well as pride in skill of needlecraft, found riotous expression in quilt-making. Women reveled in intricate and difficult patchwork; they eagerly exchanged patterns with one another; they talked over the designs and admired pretty bits of calico and pondered what combinations to make, with far more zest than women ever discuss art or examine high art specimens together today.

Today it is the old-fashioned quilt that is the new-fashioned quilt, and curiously enough, the older quilt patterns are as much at home among modern furnishings as they were among Queen Anne or Victorian designs. In our precious heirlooms we admire the crude coloring and lack of color-harmony as we do in primitive art of any time or people. There is no touch quite so modern in the present day bedroom as a lovely old patchwork quilt of grandmother's, the priceless relic of bygone days. But modern women make a study of their particular room before selecting their quilts, so the color-harmony as well as the pattern will be most suitable. A quilt in perfect harmony in one room may be exactly wrong in another.

The Victorian era was a time of warfare between puritanical restraint and unbridled emotionalism, and its influence on quilt-making was elaborateness of design—and many of the very loveliest examples of the quilt-makers' art were made during this period. The exquisite loveliness of these quilts is an inspiration for imitation and many of the oldest patterns are as beautiful, and some much more so, when made up in the soft blended colors that may be had today. A twentieth century bride may plan the color scheme for the decoration of her new home and then carry out the colors in her patchwork, both quilts and pillows. In the Colonial bedroom, where the bed was the principal piece of furniture, the quilt, often startling, yet seldom other than beautiful, was the central motif, the object of first consideration, both in pattern and coloring, and other decorations were of minor importance; hence there was no thought of matching the quilt to any particular decorative scheme. It was made of whatever the scrapbag contained, or if an especial pattern was to be copied, the materials were hand-dyed for that particular design.

In the eighteen-seventies and eighties the original "Crazy Quilt," from being the very humblest of bed coverings, was promoted to the parlor and was called a "slumber robe" or "couch throw." They were made of scraps of silks and velvets, and the more elaborately they were embroidered and hand-painted, the more elegant they were considered. I can remember the one in our pioneer home and how sorry I felt for anyone who was too poor or too shiftless to own one.

Another factor in the development of competition in beautiful quilt-making was the County Fair. Never will I forget when the "Le Moyne Star" that I pieced when I was seven years old took first prize in 1881. Life has brought me no honor to equal that one.

5

THE QUILT IN THE TWENTIETH CENTURY

THE whole country is "quilt-conscious"—the newspapers report every quilt show with glowing headlines. The Theatre has joined the throng, presenting Billy Rose's *Crazy Quilt*. Another fantasy is called *The Patchwork Quilt* and during a recent primary election in Kansas the ballot was referred to as a "Crazy Quilt"; the many names making it seem like a piece of patchwork. Later the Washington newspapers referred to the Farm Loan as a "Crazy Quilt."

The following quotation from a recently published book shows that authors, too, follow the trend of the times:

Below them on every side lay the Vermont landscape: the tumbling light green hill pastures, the deep green meadows, polka dotted here and there with clusters of buttercups and daisies; the brown-and green-striped corn fields beside dark patches of oats; the irregular stretches of woodland, dark with soft wood, light with hard wood. The whole, interlaced by gray fences and flashing brooks and tied in the corners by solitary lime trees, was spread like a giant patchwork quilt, gently sagging toward the center, on Nature's mighty quilting frames, the Adirondacks and the Green Mountains. Lake Champlain was not visible, but the fog that hung above it was like a roll of soft cotton which had escaped from a seam in the quilt. At the opposite side of the pattern, like a block of tapestry, lay the village of Greenbrook.

The making of quilts in the home has become astonishingly popular, even to the extent of interfering with bridge schedules and attendance at the matinee. One editorial writer sees in this, evidence of a well-defined reaction from woman's invasion of the business world, and suggests that her adventures into fields formerly considered man's exclusive territory are beginning to pall a little, and that she has reached back into the past for something exclusively her own. Statistics are not available at the moment to prove that this diagnosis is correct.

It's an ill depression that blows no good. Without money for costly diversions, the women have turned to a renewal of quilt-making. Many of the household magazines and not a few of the daily papers have quilt and pattern departments and are offering every inducement for the continuation of this most interesting of the home-craft arts. All this to the delight of the genuine "quilt fan"; and every quilter of distinction tells of the number of quilts she has made, especially of those that contain patches numbering into the thousands. It is of interest to know that the almanacs of the eighteen-twenties furnished quilt patterns for the edification of their readers.

A recent letter from a friend in Seattle tells of a revival of a fashion of the eighteen-eighties, the making of "Quotation Quilts." It consists of working out on bed covers clever sayings, originally designed to help while away the tedious hours when one was ill. Another friend tells of her conversion to the quilt-makers' guild: "just to watch the easy, quaint design grow under one's fingers is much more fun than playing bridge."

Quilt patterns are being "bartered" or traded in every city and community, and in one La Plata home time is just reckoned by quilt blocks. They can't have supper, or go to bed, until a quilt block is finished, and a trip to the city was postponed three days until the quilt could be set together.

What could be more fitting as a closing thought than this of Florence Bedell, of the University of Colorado: "If you wish to collect something, and every one should collect something, the quilt and the coverlet will make a most interesting and beautiful collection. Perhaps you have one to start with. Of course, associations mean much, so one from your own ancestors will be most valuable to you. With our present 'renaissance of old furniture and household articles,' the value of these bed-coverings is going up year by year. A few years ago a quilt made of pieces of dresses of Presidents' wives was offered for sale in Colorado for $25,000. If you cannot own any of these interesting things, you can at least enjoy reading and studying about them so that when the opportunity comes you can look at a collection with more appreciation."

The Thayer Museum of Art, of the University of Kansas, has a very valuable and interesting collection of quilts, a few of which are reproduced in Part II of this book.

6

HISTORICAL QUILTS FROM RECENT EXHIBITIONS

MANY quilt exhibitions are held each year in various parts of the United States, notably in the New England states, Kentucky, and the middle west—Omaha, Kansas City, Topeka, and neighboring smaller towns—and also on the Pacific Coast many cities are interested in these displays which bring together as many as six hundred or more quilts, such a bewildering scene that one cannot take in all the beauteous details. Many hundreds of dollars in prizes are awarded.

I have attended many of these exhibitions and have discussed the relative merits of the quilts on display with owners and other interested spectators. They offer a rare opportunity for the study and comparison of widely dissimilar types. The entries are usually grouped under the following heads: "Antique" (made before 1850), "Applique," "Pieced," "Unique," "Modern," and also quilts made by persons over sixty years old and by children under fourteen years of age.

At a recent "Quilt Show" sponsored by the *World-Herald,* seven hundred and thirty quilts were on display for one week and more than twenty thousands persons visited the exhibition. Some of the quilts were over one hundred years old, and one entered by Mary Belle Mattes, aged ten, was her own work. Another of unusual interest was made by Mrs. Caroline Stenius, forty-eight years ago. It is a crazy quilt and contains many "badges" that were gathered at the funeral of General Grant, in Washington, D. C.

Among the unusual quilts viewed at a recent exhibition was one that was begun before the coronation of Queen Victoria and contains approximately four thousand pieces, all from the royal dressmaker's shop in London. The present owner of the quilt has preserved its history carefully. Her own grandmother, when a small girl, visited the shop in

Tottenham Court Road where gowns for the royal family were made, and was given many bright bits of satin and silk which she later made into a quilt of intricate pattern. Many of the pieces were left-over bits from the gowns worn by Queen Victoria, the center of the quilt being arranged to contain only pieces of her court robes. The maker died before the quilt was finished and in each generation this family treasure has been inherited by the daughter who was the best needle-woman. The present owner brought the quilt with her to her home in Canada. Because it is unfinished the quilt has never been used.

History in the making is represented by a rosebud quilt made in 1772 by the great-great-grandmother of the present owner. Through necessity the quilt was literally handmade. The seed was picked from the cotton by hand and every other process from spinning and dyeing to piecing and quilting, was likewise tedious and painstaking. The colors are still bright and unfaded even after more than a century and a half, although the quilt undoubtedly saw hard wear in its early days and was frequently laundered. In recent years it has been honored as an heirloom by the present owner who lives in Paris, Tennessee.

A unique quilt was made in 1778 in Ely, England; the silk being sewed on letters written during the Revolutionary war, then in progress. The cumbersome and somewhat stilted style of letter writing of that period enhances the historical value of the ancient quilt, intriguing fragments of handwriting being discernible between the lining and the silk where the material has worn away. This quilt is the treasured possession of an ardent D.A.R.

Richard Dennis Chapter, Daughters of 1812, made a quilt which they called the "L" and it was given to Col. Charles A. Lindbergh and his bride as a wedding present. One of the members, who is a connoisseur of old quilt patterns and other historic house furnishings, found this old pattern in St. Louis about the time Col. Lindbergh flew across the Atlantic. The quilting pattern is in the form of ellipses that overlap, presenting to the imaginative mind a sketchy airplane. White and yellow sateen was used to represent air and sun.

Many fanciful effects are seen in old quilts. One had a row of hands outlined in quilting, just as if one had outlined with a pencil the outspread hand. These hands were of different shapes and sizes—evidently hands of the children in a family, and the owner's name was embroidered in the palm of each hand.

The Jolly Quilters of Lawrence, Kansas, recently put on a quilt show that was a veritable "rainbow of patchwork." This club has solved the problem of providing pleasant entertainment combined with usefulness. They have regular meeting days and each member is pledged to make at least one quilt. When the patchés for the first quilt were ready for the quilting the owner invited all the club members to her home for an old-fashioned "quilting bee." This method was continued until each member had completed her quilt and then they gave their "show," displaying the eighteen finished quilts together with some very highly prized heirlooms. One of the interesting features was a display of three quilts made by three generations of the same family, represented by Mrs. Soxman and her daughter, Crystal Soxman. The quilt made by Mrs. Soxman's mother during the Civil War was called the "French Star" with each star surrounded by sixty-four small disks. Another interesting quilt was one of original design by Mrs. J. F. Lutz, called the "Passion Flower." This was done in orchid and white. An inner wreath of colorful flowers in orchid on a white background is enclosed by a solid border of darker orchid tone. At the joining of the white center with the darker outer border, another graceful garland of flowers encircles the quilt, hundreds of leaves, buds, and blossoms being used in its making.

Another interesting quilt was one just completed by Mrs. Hoad of Lecompton, Kansas. It is an interpretation of the description by the poet, Henry Van Dyke, of "a flower within a flower and all blue." The quilt is in many shades of blue and is lined with pale blue.

At a recent quilt show given in Kansas City a silk autograph quilt was exhibited by Baroness Kurt de Pantz. It was given her by her great-grandmother, Mrs. Hire T. Wilson, a pioneer of Fort Scott, Kansas. Mrs. Wilson collected autographs of generals, poets, actors, and statesmen. She sent to each person small diamond-shaped pieces of silk on which they wrote their names in ink. These were set together with diamond-shaped blocks on which tiny flowers, violins, crests of arms, Chinese fans, and other figures were done in black on white silk. The border was handpainted in delicate floral pattern. Among the names are those of Edwin Booth, John G. Saxe, Oliver Wendell Holmes, Julia Ward Howe, Jefferson Davis, G. T. Beauregard, Chester Arthur, P. H. Sherman, and Queen Victoria. It took forty years to collect enough autographs for this quilt.

One of the most modern of quilts is that inspired by the "yo-yo" top. It is made entirely of circles of cloth about three inches in diameter. The edge is turned in and gathered round, then turned up on the top and the thread fastened so that there is a small center left open; this is filled with a bright colored bit and the round medallions are then arranged in any design you may fancy and fastened together at the edges with tiny stitches. The result is quite artistic but I remember that my mother made a "throw" of a similar design many years ago, so instead of this being a new pattern it is only an old pattern with a modern name.

A very unusual modern quilt of Colonial inspiration and feeling had an oval wreath of cherries and leaves for the center motif and a graceful festoon border of the same cherries and leaves. The cherries were in two shades of red and were stuffed, and the leaves were in three shades of green. The background was quilted in one-half inch diamonds with an artistic design of feather quilting in each corner. This was an especially designed pattern that curved out from each corner until it formed a wreath of quilting that inclosed the appliqued wreath of leaves and cherries, and was the finishing touch to a very beautiful quilt.

An unusual idea was carried out in quilting a very beautiful quilt for a hope-chest, when the prospective bridegroom drew a design or pattern of the bride-to-be's favorite flower for the white block that framed the pieced blocks. Every stitch was set by the bride and the result was much admired, but no one asked to copy it, as it was understood the pattern was to be destroyed after this one quilt was finished. But the *idea* was copied, for other prospective brides had their prospective husbands make for them accurate patterns of their own choosing for their hope-chest quilts. Leaves, linked wedding rings, stars, geometric patterns, fanciful designs, and other original ideas were carried out in the quilting, instead of using conventional designs. For borders the designs carried out the idea of flower or scroll, linked with stem or vine to match the field of the quilt.

Much publicity was given to a Quilt Contest sponsored by the Eastern States Exposition at Springfield, Massachusetts as a feature of the Annual Fair of 1932. The Town Hall of Storrowton, a New England Colonial Village on the Exposition grounds which came into being through the vision and generosity of Mrs. James J. Storrow, is the headquarters of the Home Department. Here it was, in a setting appropriately typical of an old-time New England village, that more than 700 quilts were on display. The quilts were divided into two groups—heirlooms and modern—and to each group four prizes were awarded. The first prize winner in the group of old quilts was entered by Mrs. Georgia Lewis of Fedora, South Dakota, made in 1847. But little imagination is required to picture it as having journeyed westward from New England many years ago.

The first prize award of the modern group was given to Mrs. D. T. Larimore, New York City, for uniform excellence in design, workmanship, and color harmony. This was a rose applique design with elaborate swag border and every detail of the work was done with meticulous precision and, judged as a whole, it was a perfect example of a well designed quilt, beautifully made and suitable for use in a modern room.

A quilt in a recent exhibition which has a conventional design in old-fashioned pink colonial print with a bleeding heart in the border is a copy of a quilt brought to Missouri from Virginia 71 years ago by Mrs. Martha Zion of Freeman, Missouri. Mrs. Zion is now 96 years old. The quilt was copied by Mrs. Laura Mayers, using the same colors that appear in the original quilt.

7

GLEANINGS FROM OLD SCRAPBOOKS

CRAPBOOKS have always been one of my "hobbies," and
in browsing through one that came to me recently from
a like-minded ancestor, I found an account of the wedding of
Jane Roan, daughter of the Rev. John Roan, and Mr. William
Clinger, Jr., as it was published in Dunlap's *Penna Packet* for
June 17, 1778, then published in Lancaster, Pennsylvania.

"Was married last Thursday (June 17, 1778) Mr. William Clinger,
Jr., of Donegal, to Miss Jane Roan, of Londonderry, both of Lancaster
County, a sober, sensible, agreeable young couple, and very sincere
Whigs. This marriage promises as much happiness as the state of
things in this over-sinful world will admit."

Mr. and Mrs. Clinger removed to Buffalo Valley, in Union
County, Pennsylvania, where they resided until their death.
Mr. Clinger was a prominent and influential personage on the
frontier during and subsequent to the War of the Revolution.
And we may be sure that Mrs. Clinger was a typical young
matron of that strenuous pioneer period, for in Part II, Plate
XLVI, you will find a quilt named "The Kite's Tail," which is
a nineteenth century reproduction of one that was in her
"dower-chest."

The art of needlework always has been and always will be
an attribute of femininity; soft voices, decorous manners, and
dainty fingers are associated with quilt-making, and yet, once
in a blue moon, one finds a man who is fascinated with the
artistic possibilities of the patchwork quilt. Such a man is
Charles Pratt, born of Scotch-Irish parents in Manchester,
England, in 1856, and coming to America in 1886. He claims
to be the champion quilter of the whole world, having in his
possession over two hundred letters which testify to his su-
premacy in his chosen field. He goes from state to state, to
exhibit his prize quilts, and has 393 prizes to his credit. His

first large quilt was "The Lamb of Peace" and was exhibited at the Montgomery County Fair near Philadelphia in 1911.

Another man who has won many prizes with his quilts is Charles Esterly, a farmer, living near Allentown, Pennsylvania. He believes in art for art's sake and burns the midnight oil making quilts because he loves them. He has made more than thirty, given some of them away, but never sold one. One quilt, a striking study in color, has more than nine thousand patches, each triangular in shape, with a hypotenuse of not more than one-fourth inch, sewed entirely by hand. This he considers his greatest achievement. He was once offered a considerable sum to copy one of his quilts in silk but refused, as that would take away all of his pleasure in making them.

The revival of quilt-making is a boon to many widows whose children are living in homes of their own, they being comfortably domiciled in apartment hotels where they can have comfort and convenience without care or anxiety, thus giving them leisure for all the numerous things they have always wanted to do. Mrs. E. E. Hardesty, living at the Riverside Hotel, is ninety-four years old, but she has made twenty-five quilts in recent years. As she explains: "They make such nice presents." One was being sent for a granddaughter's wedding chest. She went on to say:

When I was a girl we did not quilt any of the "tops" we had made until we were ready to be married. A girl announced her engagement by having a "quilting bee" just like you have an announcement party today.

Pointing to a marvelous example of the "Star-of-Bethlehem" quilt, she continued:

It was at the "quilting bee" for that quilt that I announced my engagement.

The thoroughness and vigor with which Victorian folk went in mourning on the least provocation is exemplified in the following article from a magazine called *Antiques*.

Mrs. Julia Ann Fleckinger (nee Cromer) was born January 8, 1827, and died October 26, 1901. During her entire life she dwelt about two miles from New Windsor, Carroll County, Maryland. From the moment when she was old enough to wield a needle and thread, she must have been an industrious piecer of quilts, for, at her death, she left one hundred and fifty quilts, one hundred of which were finished, so that each one of her four children received twenty-five quilts as a part of his inheritance. What became of the remaining fifty is not known.

Her chief title to fame, however, from a quilt lover's standpoint, lies in the fact that she made four quilts of black and white material which she used during the period of mourning following the death of her husband, and probably during other similar periods. One of these quilts is in the possession of a granddaughter, who says that it was named by the maker "midnight star." Despite its somber hues, it is attractive. The quilt measures six feet ten inches by seven feet. The five inch border is of black and white striped calico. The blocks are in "Aunt Elize's star design" and the alternating blocks are of black with a fine white line in which occur tiny spots of red and green.

Of similarly sad association is the name "coffin star" given to a combination of sixteen diamonds of alternating colors. Like so many quilt names, this one has its element of mystery. Why should a design which resembles neither a coffin nor a star be called coffin star?

Another custom in the early nineteenth century was the use of "mourning sheets" made of black linen, hand woven. As these were used only during the period of deepest mourning, it was a neighborly custom to lend them to the family in whose home bereavement made necessary all the trappings of formal mourning.

The Christian Science Monitor tells the story of the quaint old "Album" quilt recently purchased by Henry Ford for his collection of rare Americana. The recent owner, Mrs. Gertrude S. Whittlesey, granddaughter of the maker, Mrs. Benjamin Bradford Norris, of Baltimore, tells of the interesting motifs in its thirty-six blocks, no two of which are alike. Each block was made by a friend or relative and some are dated as early as 1828. The quilt gives evidence of the characters of those who made it. Each did what she could do best, or what her taste dictated. Some of the patterns are extremely intricate, others simple. Materials used range from calico to the finest plush and velvets, all appliqued onto a background of unbleached muslin. The motifs are varied, being fruits and flowers. Such fruits as cantaloupes, grapes, plums, and watermelon, all fashioned from calico, are ranged alongside of cornucopias of flowers in bewildering profusion. Tiny moss-rose buds, dainty bleeding hearts, velvet pansies, daisies, chrysanthemums, and many others, all sewed with the most microscopic of stitches.

One of the most unique of all state quilts is the Oklahoma history quilt of which Mrs. J. R. Phelan, of Oklahoma City, is the designer and maker. Obtaining pictures of persons and events in the history of the state, Mrs. Phelan first etched the design on fine cotton broadcloth, then with appropriate colors of thread she deftly embroidered each of the forty blocks that tell the story of the state's progress. The border is a clever arrangement of the flora and fauna of the state.

The first block tells of Coronado's expedition in search of gold, in 1541, wholly unaware that he was riding over the largest field of "black gold" in the world; of Napoleon signing the Louisiana purchase in 1803; of Father De Sales teaching the Indians in 1629; of the first trading post located near the present city of Muskogee in 1817; of La Harpe canoeing up the Kiamichi River in 1719.

The second block tells of Major S. H. Long consulting with the Indians in 1820; of the arrival of the Creek Indians in 1827; of the Rev. E. Campbell who established a Union Mission in 1821; of Andrew Jackson addressing the Choctaw Indians in 1832; and many other events, up to and including the present day activities of this interesting part of the "Great Middle West." It is a fitting tribute to this marvelous piece of handiwork which required three years to make, that it was considered worthy of a place among other wonders of the age at the "Century of Progress Exhibition" in Chicago, 1933.

Another quilt of historical interest in Oklahoma is the one made by forty-nine women, all of them over seventy-five years of age and most of them pioneers of Indian Territory days. When the quilt was ready for quilting these forty-nine women were the guests of Mrs. W. H. Murray, wife of the Governor, at a "quilting bee" in the executive mansion. The quilt was presented to the Oklahoma State Historical Society.

It was a New England woman, Mary Evangeline Walker, who designed a quilt of signal importance, since it was to commemorate the two hundredth anniversary of the birth of George Washington, the Father of Our Country. To accent this feature two dates are essential—1732 and 1932. The center medallion contains a profile silhouette, and the two dates which tell a tale of long years of grateful remembrance and honored appreciation. The clusters of cherries above and below the dates lend a note of whimsical pleasantry, for they recall the youthful incident of Washington and the cherry tree, which is a bit of American lore dear to all hearts. Surrounding this center block are rows of patches containing three different motifs: the hatchet, cherry tree, and Washington pavement. It is a quilt which for historical significance and intrinsic beauty appeals to every true American. (See Part II, Plate CXIX.)

The older quilt-makers seem to take special pride in making quilts of very tiny pieces so that the number will be in the thousands. A newspaper clipping tells of a Mrs. Lola Perdue in southern Missouri, who finished a quilt containing ten thousand pieces. Later the *St. Louis Post-Dispatch* tells of a Mrs. Walter Zoll, of Poplar Bluff, Missouri, who had completed a quilt that established a new world's record. The finished quilt contained twenty-one thousand, eight hundred and forty pieces. It is a unique piece of work, the small pieces being only five-eighths of an inch square. She used fifty-one spools of thread in completing her work. Later a Poplar Bluff newspaper contained the following item:

If there is an "endurance" championship for quilting, Jane Long claims it. She has made a quilt containing thirty-eight thousand pieces. When Mrs. Long heard of the quilt containing twenty-one thousand, eight hundred and forty pieces, she went to work and five months later, on her seventy-eighth birthday anniversary, she completed her quilt. She sewed it entirely by hand, using twenty spools of thread. "And not only that," she insists, "I have pieced over two hundred quilts in my time."

Back in the days when ministers were fewer and religious faith stronger, the lean form of the Reverend G. C. Warvel astride his chestnut mare was a welcome silhouette against the winter sky. And no matter how severe the weather or how difficult the roads, this dauntless man of God came bringing his message of hope and cheer to his country parishioners assembled for worship in their cross-roads churches.

For not merely to one but to six communities did this good man minister in the course of his hundred-mile circuit in the Miami, Ohio, district. And until his coming, which occurred only eight times a year at each church, were deferred the marriages and memorial services of the entire countryside. So sound was his counsel, both on temporal and spiritual matters, and so powerful and constructive an influence did he exert in the lives of the people of this vast territory that even today his name and some interesting stories of his exploits may be found on the pages of Ohio history.

It was in sincere appreciation of his services that forty women of the United Brethren Church at Miami, Ohio, in 1862 presented the Reverend Warvel with a patchwork quilt. It is intensely interesting, not only because the varied patches represent each woman's idea of beauty and symmetry, but also because of the signatures of the makers with which each block is inscribed in ink now so faded and blurred as to be almost indecipherable. The Danbys, the Pattersons, the Smiths, the Clevelands, and many other names prominent in Ohio development all are represented on the patches which make up this humble tribute to the character and deeds of a good man whose services were invaluable to this community.

The "Circuit Rider's Quilt," as it is called, is now the property of the Chicago Art Institute in their treasured collection of typical examples of early American art and needlecraft.

Claud Callan says: "The children and grandchildren soon spend the money grandpa leaves, but they hold on to the quilts grandma makes and hands down to them."

Mrs. Wilbur McCracken of Mansfield, Ohio, has made a total of 108 quilts in the past 39 years.

Hearts and Flowers! All the poesy and romanticism of an old-fashioned lace-paper valentine are embodied in the appliqued nosegays, quilted hearts, and edge scallops of an exquisite Quilted Valentine Coverlet designed by E. Marion Stevens. It is a lovely thing for a girl's room or to form part of her trousseau, for the heart motif is featured extensively in the development of the nosegays as well as in the quilting. Tiny applied hearts form the petals of many of the smaller flowers, the pendant rosy hearts of one of the favorites in grandmother's flower garden appear in the valentine bouquet and even the delicate maiden-hair fern fronds echo the same motif.

Since pink, blue, orchid, yellow, and green are combined in the treatment of the nosegays, any one of these colors may be chosen for the body of the coverlet to provide a background for the white valentine center; the coloring in the central nosegay remaining the same whatever the body color, while the smaller flowers in the border clusters are varied to harmonize with the background. Embroidery and applique are combined in the development of the nosegay motifs—all the larger flowers and leaf forms being applied and the stem and smaller ones embroidered, such stitchery as the veining on the appliqued sections being done before the patches are cut out. The central, or valentine, nosegay motif is composed of roses, daisies, asters, bleeding hearts, and bluebells combined with leaves and sprays to give an artistic arrangement. There are small clusters of the same flowers in each corner of the coverlet with still smaller clusters at intervals around the edge to form the border. Altogether it is a "thing of beauty" and should be a "joy forever."

At the ninth annual Exposition of the Women's Arts and Industries held in the Hotel Astor, an old-fashioned quilting bee was sponsored by the New York City Federation of Women's Clubs. Gold pieces and modern wool-filled quilts were offered as prizes to those turning out the neatest product. A special invitation was extended to all persons who, in earlier days, had attended quilting bees. Mrs. Alice Palmer Mitchell, eighty-five years old, the designer of the first quilt successfully manufactured by machinery, had charge of the contest.

An Associated Press dispatch calls attention to the fact that many handsome quilts, carefully stitched by busy-fingered women from Maine to California, go astray in the mails. At public auctions held by the post-office department much fine needlework is sold. Old-fashioned patchwork quilts suggesting four-posters and candle light as well as more modern appliqued designs, adorn the post-office walls for a day, then are snapped up by some woman purchaser.

One of the simplest but most effective of the colonial quilt patterns is the Double Irish Chain. One of the many institutions of which Kansas City is proud is Mercy Hospital. When the question of furnishing Nurse Hall arose, Dr. Katherine Richardson thought of the Irish Chain quilts which she remembered in her girlhood home. She visioned the homelike atmosphere these quilts would give to the rooms in the hall. Mercy Hospital is an institution that cares for crippled children; only those whose parents cannot afford to pay for such care are admitted for treatment. Because of admiration for Dr. Richardson and the wonderful work to which she devoted her life, the women of various sections of the country have organized Mercy Hospital Clubs. When word went forth that Dr. Richardson wanted Irish Chain quilts for Nurse Hall beds, these women began making Irish Chain quilts and one hundred and fifty quilts were the result of their work, all handpieced, in blue and white. The blues are the shades of the nurses' uniforms and their blue gingham house dresses. Every quilt is beautifully quilted. It is interesting to know that just about the time these quilts were finished and spread upon the beds, to the joy and satisfaction of all who saw them, Mrs. Herbert Hoover saw and admired an old colonial Irish Chain quilt. She was so delighted with it that she had it copied by a needle worker of the South and gave it to her son as one of his wedding gifts. Whatever the then new and gracious first lady of the land put her stamp of approval on, it is safe to say, carried a great deal of weight with the rest of American women.

When viewed from an airplane, fields of corn and other growing things become a great quilt suitable to tuck around a giant. From the pilot's point of view the fields of grain near Parkville, Missouri, are just a huge "Crazy Quilt." The fields of varying colored grains become the "blocks" in the patchwork and the fences are the seams and the edges of the imaginary quilt.

Why not make a National Friendship Quilt? In it you will keep the memories of friends from every state in the union. It is to be made of beautiful silk patches, each patch containing the name and the address of the friend who sent it, and be a piece of a dress she has worn. When you have collected enough patches for the quilt you will arrange them in the design you prefer and then have an old-fashioned "quilting bee" to complete it. And what a treasure chest of memories it will be in the days to come, when you can say: "Yes, granddaughter, that patch came to me from a very dear friend in Alabama. She lived on a great cotton plantation. It was her younger brother who gave your mother that cameo brooch—didn't I tell you? And this patch here! Well, a lady in Minnesota made that patch for me, years and years ago. Then her son came out to California to see us one summer——" Oh, the fun of it! Our dreams always do come true—if we have friends enough to help us work them out.

These clippings have been gathered over a period of years and the source of many of them is not known; where known, due credit has been given.

8

HOW TO MAKE A QUILT

PIECING a quilt is not so hard a task. A knowledge of plain sewing, accuracy, and neatness are all that is required. Most women today are "quilt-wise" and make a study of their particular room before selecting a quilt so the color harmony will be most suitable. A quilt becoming to one room may be exactly wrong in another. Having selected the design, the next step is to purchase a pattern, borrow one from a friend, or transfer one (using architect's tracing paper) from your favorite household magazine.

Cut the pattern of a good grade of paper, without allowing any seams, then lay the patterns on "pressboard" and cut them out actual size. This will insure a perfect pattern that will not curl up or tear and one that will last forever.

Lay the pressboard pattern on the wrong side of the material and mark around it with a well sharpened pencil. When cutting, allow for all seams and sew in the pencil mark, which will insure a perfect patch.

The two pieces to be sewed together must be accurately placed and firmly held, and the seams must be even. If you like a three-eighths inch seam, keep them all so; however, a three-sixteenths inch seam is better and all seams should be pressed flat (not open). Great care must be taken in cutting or the corners will not be true. Use a medium-sized needle, number seven or eight, and number seventy cotton thread for sewing.

Most quilts today are eighty-two by ninety inches finished for a full-sized bed and seventy-two by ninety for twin beds. From five to seven yards are required for a regular-sized quilt lining, so the top will require more to allow for the seams in the pieced quilt.

To estimate the amount of material required for each particular color in the patch, count the number of pieces of that color in the patch, then lay that pattern on a strip of paper the exact size of one-fourth yard of material. See how many patches you can cut out of this strip of paper. Multiply the number of pieces in each patch by the number of patches required for the quilt; this will give you the number of that particular color in the finished quilt. Divide the number thus obtained by the number of patches you can cut from the strip of paper, and then divide the product by four, which will give you the number of yards of that special color that you will need to buy, always allowing a little extra for "good measure" or possible accidents. Estimate each color separately.

For applique, patched, or "laid on" quilts cut your patterns and estimate your material in the same manner as for a pieced quilt, *except:* when cutting the patches lay the pressboard pattern on the *right side* of the material. This will bring the pencil marks on the right side of the material to serve as a guide in turning under the edges. Baste the colored patches onto the foundation patch in the desired design and then with a fine needle and number 100 cotton thread that has been lightly waxed, turn under and hem down all the edges. This is most interesting for there is something in the blending of colors that fascinates.

We hear so much about this "jazz age" being hard on the nerves. Quilt-making is the ideal prescription for high-tension nerves. It is soothing and there is no exercise can equal that of really creating something with the hands. And later the product of these hands may be handed down as treasured heirlooms.

There are many ways of setting a quilt together: an all-over effect of the patches, alternating the patches with squares of white, or what is known as the fence-row. The design and size of the finished patch will determine which will make the most effective quilt.

When you have finished your "top" turn it over to an experienced quilter, for a beautiful quilt may be made or marred by the quilting. Most professional quilters charge per "spool" with an extra charge for marking, also a charge for binding.

Oh, don't you remember the babes in the wood,
Who were lost and bewildered and crying for food,
And the robins who found them, thinking them dead,
Covered them over with leaves brilliant red
And russet and orange and silver and gilt?
Well! that was the very first crazy-patch quilt.

FLO E. FLINTJER.

PLATE I

9

REPRODUCTIONS OF QUILT PATCHES

PLATE I

No. 1—This is a sample of original American patchwork as conceived by our early Colonial mothers. With the frugality necessary in the early days of our country, they cut from worn and discarded woolen clothing the patches of material yet intact and considered useful, and sewed them together "crazy fashion" and with a back and padding or interlining, fastened them together at intervals with stitches of vari-colored yarn in the manner known as "knotting a comforter." This is an all-over pattern.

No. 2—This is the nineteenth century development of "Crazy" patch-work, when silks and velvets were basted upon a cambric foundation, the edges being held together with various embroidery stitches. The more elaborate the handiwork the more beautiful the finished quilt. They were usually made in large-sized squares and then sewed together to make an all-over effect. These were used as "slumber robes" or "couch throws." (See Part II, Plate XXX and Plate LXXI.)

No. 3—This is the twentieth century development of the "crazy" quilt in cotton pieces. Small scraps of colored prints are sewed together in an irregular design; then cut into regular shaped pieces set together with a diamond design in plain color. This is colonial in inspiration but modern in usage.

No. 4—The original "Four-patch." Change is the result of all prog-ress. One of our colonial ancestors, having a flair for variety, decided to cut her patches by a regular shaped pattern instead of using them in the irregular form. The three basic designs earliest used were the square, the rectangle, and the diamond. In the four-patch we see the very simplest form of the square, the design being created by the use of light and dark patches. Secondary designs are the hexagon and the circle. These five designs and the various parts into which they may be divided form the entire range of lines in quilt-pattern cutting.

PLATE 00

No. 5—This is another variation of the "Four-patch."

No. 6—The "Nine-patch" in its simplest form was the next step in the use of the square patch and the one oftenest used for the child's first lesson in quilt-making. (See Part II, Plate XCI.) The Nine-patch is of Massachusetts origin. For all their industrious ways, New England women read, attended church gatherings and singing school, held education in high esteem, and shared in the general life of the community. New England patterns were more pictorial but not so intricate as those of the Pennsylvania Dutch.

No. 7—The "Leavenworth Nine-patch," a modern arrangement of colored patches, named for her home town by Carrie A. Hall.

No. 8—The "Tonganoxie Nine-patch," another variation named in honor of the Ladies' Association of the Congregational Church of Tonganoxie.

No. 9—This is a very lovely twentieth century variation of the "Nine-patch" which makes a beautiful all-over quilt.

Nos. 10 and 11—Two variations called "Double Nine-patch."

No. 12—The "Split Nine-patch."

Nos. 13, 14, 15, and 16—All variations of the original "Nine-patch." The design is created by the different size of the patches and by the arrangement of colors.

PLATE II

EACH STITCH

The stitches in this quilt-patch rare,
Were patiently made with loving care;
If each thought put forth were as perfect and true,
It would make a grand world for me and you.

IDA H. FREDERICK.

Work which grows beautiful under one's own hands is truly a pleas-
ure, and what more so than the making of a patchwork quilt?

PLATE II

No. 1—Called "Hit and Miss," shows the use of the rectangular patch when scraps are plentiful. An all-over pattern. "Hit and Miss," "Roman Stripe," and "Brick Wall" are known as the "One-patch." The square cut diagonally in half and arranged to form a pattern was called a "Two-patch."

Nos. 2 and 3—Known as "Brick Work" show an arrangement of all print patches in the well known manner of brick laying with muslin patches used to give a more decorative effect.

Nos. 4, 5, and 6—These are variations of the well-loved "Log Cabin" pattern. No Colonial home was complete without one or more of these geometrical arrangements of scraps. Oftenest made of woolen pieces, treasured indeed were those made of scraps of silk and pieces cut from silk dresses that were past even "second best" wearing. The placement of light and dark pieces in setting together the square block created various designs known as "Barn Raising" and "Straight Furrow." (See Part II, Plate XLVII and Plate LXII.)

Nos. 7 and 8—A modern variation of the same pattern, called "Fine Woven" and "Coarse Woven" patchwork.

No. 9—"Roman Stripe." Rectangular scraps of silk of varying widths are sewed together into strips and set together lengthwise with strips of black silk cut from the voluminous skirts of discarded silk dresses.

No. 10—"Roman Square." The same rectangular patch with a square effect produced by the division lines of black. (See Part II, Plate XCVII.) This is the best known example of the "Three-patch."

Nos. 11 and 12—"Cube Work" and "Baby Blocks" introducing the diamond motif and showing the infinite possibilities of the creative mind. The diamond was a special favorite in New England and they used it for their best quilts. "Baby Blocks" must be carefully pieced on account of the corners coming exactly together to produce that charming but puzzling geometric effect.

No. 13—"Zig-Zag," "Streak-of-Lightning," or "Rail Fence." Here we have the diamond cut crosswise, forming a triangle, the arrangement of light and dark giving the zig-zag effect.

No. 14—"Ice Cream Bowl." The triangular shaped pieces give the effect of cut glass.

No. 15—"Economy patch."

No. 16—"Right and Left." An all-over pattern.

No. 17—"Octagon."

No. 18—"Postage Stamp" (actual size). An all-over design that is economical but not beautiful.

The last four patterns were designed to use the very smallest pieces in the scrap-bag.

PLATE III

Some variation of the diamond or square forms the base of all star patterns, which far outnumber all other designs, more than one hundred being shown in these plates. The simplest form is an eight-pointed star known as the "Star-of-LeMoyne." This is of French origin. The Le-Moyne brothers were given a grant of land in 1699 known as Louisiana and in 1718 they founded the city of New Orleans. In the New England states the name was shortened to "Lemon Star."

PLATE III

No. 1—"Star-of-LeMoyne." All "Lily" and "Tulip" designs are based on this famous pattern.

No. 2—"Star-of-North Carolina."

Nos. 3 and 4—Both these designs, though so unlike, are called the "Evening Star."

No. 5—The "Pieced Star." Designed to use small scraps.

No. 6—"Star-of-the-West."

No. 7—"Slashed Star" of intricate design but very beautiful; the colors radiate from deep orange in the center to pale yellow at the end of the rays.

No. 8—"Starlight."

No. 9—"Texas Star."

No. 10—"Geometric Star."

No. 11—"Patty's Star."

No. 12—"Stars and Squares," also "Rising Star."

No. 13—"Pin-wheel Star."

No. 14—"Brunswick Star," "Rolling Star," or "Chained Star."

No. 15—"Seven Stars." Offers many interesting possibilities and makes a very attractive quilt when set together with triangles of the light material with a fitted quilting motif.

Nos. 16 and 17—These are both called "Star-of-Bethlehem," yet they are unlike in design. No. 17 is an original design by Carrie A. Hall.

PLATE IV

. . . blossomed the lovely stars, the forget-me-nots of the angels.
LONGFELLOW'S *Evangeline.*

PLATE IV

No. 1—"Dolly Madison's Star." Dolly Madison was the first "Mistress of the White House" with social consciousness and the only one who held that title for sixteen years. The design of Virginia origin in the early nineteenth century, developed in red, white, and blue, was very appropriate, signifying the new Republic.

No. 2—Simple "Five-point Star."

No. 3—"Star-of-the-West." Also "Compass" and "The Four Winds."

No. 4—"King's Star."

No. 5—"Feather Star," also "Twinkling Star," "Star-of-Bethlehem," and "Saw Tooth." When it is pieced with a hexagon in the center it becomes a "Radiant Star" and with a nine-patch in the center it is called a "California Star." Also sometimes called a "Chestnut Burr." (See Part II, Plates X, XI, and LIX.)

No. 6—"Missouri Star"; also "Shining Star." This pattern requires concentration. It will be of interest to quilters to know that this pattern was designed by a man, because of a real interest in geometric figures and composition.

No. 7—"Christmas Star."

Nos. 8, 9, and 10—These three stars are all cut by the same pattern. The difference in design is due to the arrangement of color. No. 8, "Variable Star," No. 9, "Lone Star" or "Texas Star," No. 10, "Ohio Star." Note the design in white with color used as a background.

No. 11—"Enigma Star."

No. 12—"Hexagonal Star." Called "Rising Star" in northern New York in 1825.

No. 13—"Union Star." White star, blue field, and red border.

Nos. 14 and 15—Both called "Blazing Star." Each beautiful in design and yet very different.

No. 16—"Cluster-of-Stars," an all-over pattern. Note the squares of printed material used to set the patches together gives a most pleasing effect.

PLATE V

. . . As stars to thee appear
Seen in the galaxy, that milky way
Which nightly as a circling zone thou seest
Powdered with stars.
MILTON'S *Paradise Lost.*

PLATE V

No. 1—"Virginia Star"; also "Star-upon-Stars."

No. 2—"Star-of-Chamblie." An antique design brought to Canada from France in the early part of the nineteenth century. Developed in red, orange, green, and white.

No. 3—"Four-pointed Star"; also "Blazing Star." (See Plate IV, Nos. 14 and 15.)

No. 4—"Odd Star."

Nos. 5 and 6—"St. Louis Star." The same name but different in design.

No. 7—"Jackson Star"; also "Four Stars."

No. 8—"Star-of-the-East." Originated in Kentucky.

No. 9—"Rolling Star."

No. 10—"Aunt Eliza's Star." Note the design in white with figured background.

No. 11—"Mexican Star." An all-over pattern. Recently a quilt collector found a beautiful old "Mexican Star" quilt up in the mountains of New York. It was a handsome specimen in reds and blues. These same lovely patterns being found in the north, south, east, and west testify to the far-flung ties that bound together the scattered settlers of Mexican War days when this pattern was doubtless originated.

No. 12—"Royal Star."

No. 13—"French Star."

No. 14—"Beautiful Star." Variety is unlimited in the field of quilt patterns; that is one secret of the fascination which continues from generation to generation.

No. 15—"Pontiac Star" is a very pretty star pattern because of its arrowhead motif. The stars are placed in a very interesting arrangement. In putting the quilt together watch the position of the stars very carefully.

No. 16—"Chicago Star."

No. 17—"Premium Star."

No. 18—"Star-of-Hope."

No. 19—"Tiny Star." An all-over pattern, every piece being cut by the one small diamond pattern. Six diamonds make the star and three diamonds form the white hexagon.

No. 20—"Arrowhead Star"; also "Star-of-Many-Points."

No. 21—"Tennessee Star."

PLATE VI

Innumerable as the stars of night,
Or stars of morning, dewdrops which the sun
Impearls on every leaf and every flower.
MILTON'S *Paradise Lost.*

PLATE VI

No. 1—"Iowa Star."

No. 2—"Modernistic Star." Thoroughly modern in interpretation and execution.

No. 3—"Falling Star"; also called "Flying Star," "Flying Swallow," and "Circling Swallows." A great favorite in New England and Pennsylvania—c. 1800.

Nos. 4, 5, and 6—These are called "Morning Star," showing how the same name may be applied to entirely different designs in different localities. The design in most patches is carried out in the print or color while the white is used as the background. It is the exception that proves the rule. Note No. 5: This is an all-over pattern and the completed quilt could be a blue print of small design scattered over with scintillating white stars. The name, "Morning Star," suggests the quiet hour just before the break of dawn; No. 4 would be most effective in a color combination suggesting dawn.

No. 7—"Hunter's Star." An all-over pattern.

No. 8—"Diamond Star."

No. 9—"Cowboy's Star"; also "Arkansas Traveler," or "Travel Star." c. 1860.

No. 10—"Four X Star." The four X design forms the corners of the patch, being emphasized by using plain color.

No. 11—"Star and Cross."

No. 12—"King David's Crown," one of the more simple patterns taking its name from the Bible which was often used because of its easy construction.

No. 13—"Double Star"; also "Star-within-a-Star," and "Carpenter's Wheel."

No. 14—"Ring-Around-the-Star"; also "Star and Chains" and "Rolling Star."

No. 15—"Savannah Beautiful Star."

No. 16—"Starry Lane."

No. 17—"Octagonal Star," also called "Dutch Rose."

No. 18—"Braced Star."

PLATE VII

Till the sun grows cold, and the stars are old
And the leaves of the Judgment Book unfold.
BAYARD TAYLOR.

PLATE VII

No. 1—"Star Puzzle."

No. 2—"Chinese Star."

No. 3—"Old Colony Star."

No. 4—"New Star." An all-over pattern. When four patches are sewed together the star is developed, and so on—all over the quilt.

No. 5—"Oriental Star."

No. 6—"Prairie Star," also "Harvest Sun" in the Middle West. In Massachusetts it is known as the "Ship's Wheel."

No. 7—"Columbia Star."

No. 8—"Persian Star."

No. 9—"Mother's Fancy Star."

No. 10—"Flower Star."

No. 11—"Modern Star."

No. 12—"Twinkling Star" or "Star and Crescent" of Pennsylvania Dutch origin. These people despised book-learning for women; hence their devotion to the household arts and their pride in their intricate patterns and the skill with which they were executed. Their quilts were highly individualistic.

No. 13—"Leavenworth Star."

No. 14—"Kansas Star." Original design by Harold Fisher. An all-over pattern. The effect of the finished quilt is a succession of four-pointed stars. The smallest ones are deep orange, the medium sized ones yellow, and the largest ones are brown.

No. 15—"Eccentric Star."

No. 16—"Polaris Star"; also "Flying Bat."

No. 17—"Arabian Star"; also "Dutch Tile."

No. 18—"Lucinda's Star." Indiana c. 1850. (See Part II, Plate IV.)

PLATE VIII

Their religion was such a vital part of the lives of our ancestors that it is not strange they gave Bible names to so many quilt patches.

PLATE VIII

No. 1—"Job's Troubles"; also called "Four-Point," "Kite," and "Snowball."

No. 2—"Job's Tears" in 1800. In 1825 it became the "Slave Chain," showing the tendency of the times, when slavery and not religion was the paramount issue of the day. In 1840 when Texas was the topic in everyone's thought this pattern became "Texas Tears." After the Civil War it was called "The Rocky Road to Kansas" or "Kansas Troubles," and finally it became the "Endless Chain." An all-over design.

Nos. 3, 9, and 14—"Robbing-Peter-to-Pay-Paul." This is a very old Quaker name and has been applied to many different patterns.

No. 4—"Garden of Eden."

No. 5—"Cross"; modern.

Nos. 6 and 7—"Cross and Crown," of Colonial origin. No. 6 is a bizarre design common only to the community in which it originated. There are many such and the present generation of quilters have added their quota to those of the past.

No. 8—"Crown of Thorns"; also "Georgetown Circle," "Single Wedding Ring," and "Memory Wreath." When called "Memory Wreath" it was made of pieces of dresses worn by the dear departed, the name and date of death being embroidered in the white center square.

No. 10—"The Delectable Mountains," one of the most pleasing of designs. It is a delight to the eye of the beholder and brings a warmth of patriotism to the heart when one realizes all that it meant to John Bunyan's pilgrims and to the Pilgrims who landed on the barren shores of America in search of peace *ad libitum*. This patch shows the center of the quilt. The pieced triangles continue in rows around this center until the quilt is completed.

No. 11—"Wonder of the World."

No. 12—"Ecclesiastical."

No. 13—"Joseph's Coat." A patch of many colors which will use up every scrap in the bag, in fact, it is called "Scrap-bag" in Pennsylvania.

No. 15—"King David's Crown."

No. 16—"Children of Israel."

No. 17—"World Without End," from the Book of Common Prayer was, as it still is, a phrase familiar in every church no matter of what creed. It is also called "Priscilla." An all-over pattern, the light and dark colors being alternated in every other block.

No. 18—"Golgotha"; also called "The Three Crosses" and "Cross upon Cross."

No. 19—"Coronation"; also called "King's Crown." This name dates back to the days of Sir Walter Raleigh and the gallant knights of old, but in New England the design became known as "Coronation." Later, "President's Quilt," "Washington's Quilt," and "Potomac Pride." c 1830.

No. 20—"Jacob's Ladder." An all-over pattern and one of the most striking of quilts having Bible names.

No. 21—"David and Goliath" has several other names: "Four Darts," "Bull's Eye," "Flying Darts," "Doe and Darts"—all having similar association of the hunt or archery. The older the pattern the more likely it is to have many names, showing that it has migrated from one community to another and has taken its successive names from association with various incidents in the history and development of home life in America.

No. 22—"Jacob's Ladder." Of New England interpretation and pre-Revolutionary origin, cut by the same pattern as No. 20 but a different arrangement of colors. In New England and Virginia it is called "Stepping Stones"; in Pennsylvania, "The Tail of Benjamin's Kite"; in Mississippi and the prairie states, "Trail of the Covered Wagon" or "Wagon Tracks"; and in western Kentucky, the "Underground Railroad." An all-over pattern.

PLATE IX

Patchwork has nothing to do with "crosspatches" and yet many patches have names in which "cross" plays the leading rôle. These owe their origin to the intensely religious life of the times.

PLATE IX

Nos. 1 and 15—"Maltese Cross." Two variations of this interesting pattern. No. 15 is also called "Pineapple."

No. 2—"Royal Cross."

No. 3—"Cross-within-a-Cross."

Nos. 4 and 11—"King's Crown." Two interpretations of the same pattern.

No. 5—"Crowned Cross"; also "Cross and Crown."

No. 6—"Odd Fellows' Cross."

No. 7—"Roman Cross."

No. 8—"Queen's Crown."

No. 9—"Cæsar's Crown."

Nos. 10 and 13—"Greek Cross." Two patches of the same name. One of the variations of the original nine-patch and a great favorite early in the nineteenth century.

No. 12—"Steps-to-the-Altar."

No. 14—"Cross and Crown." This quaint old pattern with its firm-in-the-faith title is really a variation of the lily blocks which have flowers resembling these "crowns."

Nos. 16 and 19—"Red Cross." Two interpretations of a well known emblem.

No. 17—"Crosses and Losses"; also "Fox and Geese." With just a slight variation this pattern becomes "Hovering Hawks" or "Triple X" and with still further rearrangements, the "Anvil" and the "Swallow." (See Part II, Plate VI.)

No. 18—"Queen Charlotte's Crown," named by the women of Virginia in compliment to the wife of George III. After 1770, it was called "Indian Meadow."

No. 20—"Old King Cole's Crown."

PLATE X

Day after day the pattern grew;
Each block was deftly set in place,
And rows of tiny stitches tell
A tale that time cannot efface.
Of patience, skill, housewifely pride,
Of women's love for pretty things,
Of fingers trained such work to do
By those who know the joy it brings,
Of time within the home well spent,
The heart with homely tasks content.

From *The Patchwork Coverlet.*

PLATE X

No. 1—"Duck Paddle," or "Fanny's Fan."

No. 2—"String of Beads." Very modern. An all-over pattern.

No. 3—"Rebecca's Fan." The "fan" as a motif for quilt patterns was very popular in our grandmothers' day. No lady was properly gowned for a social function unless the ensemble included a fan.

No. 4—"Dutchman's Puzzle," an adaptation of the "Wind Mill"—a favorite about 1820.

No. 5—"Caroline's Fan," a modern design with Colonial feeling.

No. 6—"Flo's Fan."

No. 7—"Grandmother's Fan."

No. 8—"Old Maid's Puzzle." A genuine antique, for there haven't been any "old maids" for several generations, and "bachelor girls" are not easily puzzled.

No. 9—"Churn Dash," one of the prettiest of the four-patch designs. The source of many of the quilt names was found in the trades and occupations of the times.

No. 10—"Double Hearts"; also "St. Valentine's Patch."

No. 11—"Spinning Triangles."

No. 12—"Sister's Choice." The simple contacts of everyday family life are responsible for many of their quilt names.

No. 13—"Children's Delight."

No. 14—"True Lover's Knot." In Kentucky it was called the "Sassafras Leaf"; in New England, the "Hand"; and in the Middle West the "California Oak Leaf."

No. 15—"Pullman Puzzle"; also "Baseball" and "Snowball."

No. 16—"Puss-in-the-Corner. c 1855.

No. 17—"Grandmother's Choice."

No. 18—"Jack-in-the-Box"; also "Whirligig."

No. 19—"Clay's Choice." Quilt patterns are ever so much more interesting if one knows their stories. This is a very lovely block in its own right but when it is traced back to the bitter days of Calhoun and Clay one finds it had other names—"Harry's Star," "Henry of the West," and "Star of the West."

No. 20—"Aunt Sukey's Choice."

No. 21—"Lovers' Links," an all-over pattern.

No. 22—"Eternal Triangle" is the antique name, the modern name is "Merry-go-Round."

No. 23—"Triangular Triangles."

PLATE XI

Picked out in colors which the tone of time
Alone can give, old Neptune's mighty swell
Is pictured here, with many a lovely shell,
In needlework symmetrical as rhyme!

AMY SMITH.

PLATE XI

No. 1—"Double Star." A modern design of great beauty.

No. 2—"Milky Way"—a variation of the "Indiana Puzzle."

No. 3—"Dove-in-the-Window." This is rather an intricate pattern to piece but a charming and unusual one when finished.

No. 4—"Rockingham's Beauty." Modern.

No. 5—"Ocean Wave." One of the authentic old-fashioned quilt patterns with a tang of the sea which shows its coastwise ancestry. It was a decided favorite with those who wished to put considerable piecing into the making of a beautiful quilt. It is an all-over pattern and one can readily see "ocean waves" in the completed quilt.

No. 6—"Dutch Mill.

Nos. 7 and 10—"Kaleidoscope." These patches are very appropriately named as there is a great variety of symmetrical colored pieces in their different forms.

No. 8—"Wind Mill," "Water Wheel," "Mill Wheel," and all similar patterns are variations of the original "Wind Mill.'

No. 9—"Bachelor's Puzzle."

No. 11—"Blue Birds." A modern arrangement of many diamonds, forming a hexagon patch.

No. 12—"Hexagon"; can be arranged very effectively as an all-over or set together with triangles of a third color.

No. 13—"Butterfly," a favorite old-time pattern.

No. 14—"Duck and Ducklings," also called "Corn and Beans," "Handy Andy," "Hen and Chickens," and "Shoo-fly."

No. 15—"Cactus Flower," an interesting variation of the old "Maple Leaf" motif and suggestive of the Southwest.

No. 16—"Kitty-Corner" or "Puss-in-the-Corner." In 1811 it was called "Tic-Tac-Toe."

No. 17—"Grecian Design."

No. 18—"Bird-of-Paradise."

No. 19—"Swallow."

No. 20—"Prairie Queen."

No. 21—"Cats and Mice." Of Pennsylvania Dutch origin.

No. 22—"Clam Shell," a Cape Cod design more often used as a quilting design than in actual patchwork. Intricate to piece but very effective when finished.

No. 23—"Hen and Chickens."

PLATE XII

Stories of the origin of quilt names are numerous. This song is said to be responsible for several.

When the "Swallows" homeward fly,
When the "Roses" scattered lie,
When from neither hill nor dale
Chants the silvery nightingale;
In these words my "Bleeding Heart"
Would to thee its grief impart.

PLATE XII

No. 1—"Steeple Chase"; also "Bows and Arrows."

No. 2—"Turkey Tracks."

No. 3—"Goose Tracks."

No. 4—"Goose-in-the-Pond." In 1810 called "Young Man's Fancy." (See Part II, Plate LXXXV.)

No. 5—"Bird's Nest."

No. 6—"Swallows-in-a-Window."

No. 7—"Dove of Peace." The dove being the quilting design—an all-over pattern of great beauty when completed.

No. 8—Mrs. Keller's "Nine-patch."

No. 9—"Flock of Geese." Very old Colonial pattern.

Nos. 10 and 13—"Chimney Swallows." Somewhat similar to "Coronation."

No. 11—"Springtime Blossoms" has many names: "Lazy Daisy," "Petal Quilt," and "Wheel-of-Fortune." Each quilter will use it as her fancy dictates both as to color combination and name.

No. 12—"Hovering Hawks."

No. 14—"Anvil."

No. 15—"Wandering Foot"; also "Turkey Tracks." As the "Wandering Foot" was supposed to have a malign influence, no child was allowed to sleep under one, else he would grow up discontented, unstable, and of a roving disposition. No bride would have one in her dower-chest. Later the name was changed to "Turkey Tracks" to break the curse. Developed in green on a white foundation it is called "Iris Leaf."

No. 16—"Dogwood Blossoms." These two patches, developed in a pale green figured print and white alternate in an all-over pattern and make a very beautiful quilt.

No. 17—"Crow's Foot."

PLATE XIII

Grannie sits in her oaken chair
The firelight flits o'er her silvery hair,
The silent children around her sit,
As she pieces her patchwork coverlet;
She tells them her story of London Town,
And shows them the scraps of her bridal gown;
Each fragment there is a printed page,
With mem'ries written 'twixt youth and age.
                    From the old song, *Patchwork.*

PLATE XIII

No. 1—"Ornate Star"; also "Combination Star."

No. 2—"Rolling Stone" or "Block Circle" or "Johnnie-round-the-Corner."

No. 3—"W. C. T. U." Should be developed in blue and white.

No. 4—"Road-to-Oklahoma"; also, "New Four-patch."

No. 5—"Arrowheads."

Nos. 6 and 10—"Chips and Whetstones." Very old patterns. No. 10 has several other names but none so quaint as this one.

No. 7—"Cross Roads."

No. 8—"Stars and Planets."

Nos. 9 and 18—"Georgetown Circle." No. 9 is a combination of "Star" and "Wreath" patterns and No. 10 is also called "Crown of Thorns," "Single Wedding Ring," and when made of pieces of the dresses of a loved one who has passed on it is called "Memory Wreath" and the name and date of death is embroidered in the center square.

No. 11—"Indian Trails." This pattern has as many as fourteen different names. "Forest Path," "Rambling Road," "North Wind," "Irish Puzzle," "Winding Walk," "Old Maid's Ramble," "Storm-at-Sea," and several others, depending upon the locality where you find the quilt. "Indian Trails" seems most appropriate because of the unmistakable Swastika emblem in the block. Then, too, this pattern originated in the early days when the settlers were gradually moving westward and their contact with the Indians greatly influenced their daily lives.

No. 12—"Ozark Diamond"; also "Ozark Star." Hexagons, triangles, and diamonds go together to make this most fascinating patch. It is one in which the ingenuity of the quilter may be put to effective use, for an unusually large number of color combinations are possible.

No. 13—"Mary Tenny Gray Travel Club Patch." All roads lead toward the center, the home of the Club.

No. 14—"Log Cabin Star." The diamonds are pieced of small strips, then cut and pieced to form the star.

No. 15—"Rocky-Road-to-Kansas." The four-pointed star is made of irregular shaped pieces sewed together "Crazy" fashion, then cut into points using white as a background.

No. 16—"Windmill Star"; also "Amethyst." February is the month of famous birthdays, Lincoln's Washington's and Lindbergh's, and the amethyst is its jewel, thus making an especially appropriate pattern for a birthday quilt.

No. 17—"Diamond and Star."

No. 19—"Royal Star."

No. 20—"Star Flower" or "Golden Glow."

No. 21—"Circular Saw," an old-time pattern, also called "Oriole Window" and "Four Little Fans."

No. 22—"Sail Boat." The name shows its coastwise origin.

No. 23—"Octagonal Star."

No. 24—"Pickle Dish."

PLATE XIV

The simple pleasures of the every-day life of the colonists and their close touch with nature are reflected in their quilt-patch names. Great-grandmother had no movies, no automobiles, no airplanes, no radios; is it any wonder she wove her pleasures into patchwork quilts?

PLATE XIV

No. 1—"Mollie's Choice."

No. 2—"Gold Fish" or "Fish Block." Of New England origin, a modification of the "Dove-in-the-Window" design. Usually it takes a vivid imagination to guess why our designing ancestors bestowed on their creations of squares and triangles such fanciful names, but in this pattern one can almost smell the salt water. If you have not the deep-sea eye for discovering marine life in calico, you still may appreciate a most rhythmical and conventional design.

No. 3—"Ladies' Delight."

No. 4—"Sunbeam." Transforming sunbeams into a radiantly beautiful quilt is an achievement worth while.

No. 5—"Sunburst." A sunburst quilt means much work to the block, but very few blocks to the quilt. This is most effective when the blocks are set diagonally into the quilt, for this would require half-blocks to fill in the edge, producing an effect like great rising or setting suns.

No. 6—"Honey Bee." A charming example of combining piecing and applique. It is a bit less trouble to piece the entire block and applique the bee's wings and bodies afterward. (See Part II, Plate LVI), also called "Blue Blazes."

Nos. 7 and 13—"Spider Web." Two interpretations of the same name. No. 7 may be used as an all-over pattern or set together with same size squares of white. No. 13 is set together with triangles of white.

No. 8—"Golden Glow." Modern.

No. 9—"Corn and Beans," "Shoo-fly," "Handy Andy," "Hen and Chickens," or "Duck and Ducklings." This was the pattern used for a quilt that was on the bed in the first "Farm Demonstration Home," in Missouri, which attests its popularity.

No. 10—"Old Maid's Ramble."

No. 11—"Mrs. Cleveland's Choice"; also "County Fair."

No. 12—"Clown's Choice."

No. 14—"Grandmother's Favorite."

No. 15—"Bat's Wings."

No. 16—"Rising Sun" is an intricate pattern, but not enough so to daunt the quilter who aspires to a design both beautiful and unusual. There are several variations of the "Rising Sun," both pieced and appliqued.

No. 17—"Jack-in-the-Pulpit" or "Toad-in-the-Puddle."

No. 18—"Snow Ball."

No. 19—"Rainbow."

No. 20—"Bear's Paw" in western Pennsylvania and Ohio in 1850. In Long Island called "Duck's Foot-in-the-Mud," and it is not surprising that the Quakers of Philadelphia called it the "Hand-of-Friendship."

PLATE XV

Glad memories are woven unawares
In blending pieces of each favorite dress!
And so this quilt is eloquent today
With happiness that passes not away.
                                    AMY SMITH.

PLATE XV

No. 1—"Chinese Puzzle," an all-over design. The lines of dark forming a very striking effect in the finished quilt.

No. 2—"Crossword Puzzle." Modern.

No. 3—"Yankee Puzzle," a favorite in New York and the New England states.

No. 4—"Irish Puzzle" or "Kansas Troubles," an all-over design.

No. 5—"Indiana Puzzle," an intricate all-over pattern, very famous in pioneer days in Indiana. It is remarkably effective, considering the simplicity of the patches, and makes a striking quilt. (See Part II, Plate XXII.)

No. 6—"Missouri Puzzle."

No. 7—"Puss-in-the-Corner" or "Puss-in-Boots."

No. 8—"Tile Puzzle."

No. 9—"Columbia Puzzle."

No. 10—"Thelma's Choice."

No. 11—"Devil's Puzzle" or "Fly Foot," a favorite with our great-grandmothers.

No. 12—"Mrs. Morgan's Choice."

No. 13—"Bow-Knot" or "Farmer's Puzzle" was a favorite in the eighteenth century—the design is very similar to the "Swastika."

No. 14—"Fanny's Favorite," an intricate design that is beautiful and shows Fanny was a woman of more than average artistic sensibility.

No. 15—"Bachelor's Puzzle."

PLATE XVI

How much piecin' a quilt is like livin' a life! You can give the same kind of pieces to two persons, and one will make a "nine-patch" and one'll make a "wild goose chase," and there will be two quilts made out of the same kind of pieces, and jest as different as they can be. And that is jest the way with livin'. The Lord sends us the pieces, but we can cut them out and put 'em together pretty much to suit ourselves, and there's a heap more in the cuttin' out and the sewin' than there is in the caliker."

ELIZA CALVERT HALL in *Aunt Jane of Kentucky.*

PLATE XVI

No. 1—"Memory Block," often made of pieces of different dresses of a child or of some other loved member of the family, as a "keepsake" and in after years each piece was pointed to with pride.

No. 2—"Fence Row."

Nos. 3 and 7—"Beggar's Blocks." These interesting patterns hark back to the neighborly custom of begging one's friends for scraps of their dresses or men's old neckties to put into a quilt. No. 7 was called "Cats and Mice" by the Pennsylvania Dutch.

No. 4—"Hour Glass."

No. 5—"Necktie." This shows that the Colonial women were very considerate of the men-folk of their families.

No. 6—"Goblet."

No. 8—"Devil's Claws."

No. 9—"Crown of Thorns"; also "New York Beauty" and "Rocky Mountain Road." This is only one fourth of the finished block.

No. 10—"Indian Hatchet," "Tree Everlasting," "Follow the Leader," and "Crazy Ann" are all so suggestive of the modernistic decoration of the present day that a modern bedroom with its "futuristic" furniture would be enhanced by one of these folk-craft creations.

No. 11—"Sugar Loaf."

No. 12—"Pyrotechnics" a very intricate and beautiful design not to be undertaken except by an experienced quilter.

No. 13—"Sugar Bowl," called the "Fly" in Ohio; "Kathy's Ramble" in New York; "Crow's Foot" in Maryland, and "Fan Mill" in Pennsylvania.

Nos. 14 and 19—"Handy Andy." Two patches of the same name but different in design.

No. 15—"Barrister's Block" or "Lawyer's Puzzle" of New England origin, a first cousin, once removed, of "Irish Puzzle" or "Kansas Troubles."

No. 16—"Propeller." Very modern.

No. 17—"Air Plane."

No. 18—"Tile Patchwork."

No. 20—"Compass" offers a fascinating number of designs, chief of which is a perfect "Maltese Cross," formed when four blocks are sewed together.

No. 21—"Aircraft." Modern.

No. 22—"All Kinds," an interesting block despite its name.

No. 23—"Brick Pile."

No. 24—"Octagon Tile."

PLATE XVII

Variety is truly unlimited and is one of the secrets of quilt fascination which charms from generation to generation; it afforded a means of expression of individuality and originality in the life of the lonely New England woman and the isolated mountain woman of Kentucky.

PLATE XVII

No. 1—"Secret Drawer." This name brings to memory the old story about long lost wills that, when found, brought great wealth, or perhaps it will remind you of mother's hiding place for odd bits of old jewelry which we were allowed to see on special occasions, or as a reward of merit. This pattern is also called "Spools" and in Arkansas it is called the "Arkansaw Traveler."

No. 2—"Little Saw Tooth"; also "Lend and Borrow," "Rocky Glen," "Indian Meadow," and "Lost Ship."

No. 3—"Stepping Stones."

Nos. 4 and 5—"Whirligig." Two patches having the same name but entirely different in design.

No. 6—"Crazy Ann."

No. 7—"Yankee Pride" or "Maple Leaf."

No. 8—"Four H Club Patch." Colors green and white.

No. 9—"World's Fair." This perpetuates the grandeur of the great exposition held in Chicago in 1893.

No. 10—"Patience Corners." A combination of squares and diamonds in an all-over pattern that was very popular in the last half of the eighteenth century.

No. 11—"Farmer's Wife."

No. 12—"Double X."

No. 13—"Letter X."

No. 14—"Baby Bunting." This most elaborate all-over quilt pattern with its cunning name will afford even the experienced quilter a new thrill in the combination of colors and blocks.

No. 15—"X-quisite," an all-over pattern.

No. 16—"Snail's Trail," an all-over pattern.

No. 17—"Monkey Wrench," an all-over pattern also called "Snail's Trail" in some localities. It is a first cousin to the "Indiana Puzzle."

No. 18—"Arabic Lattice," an all-over pattern.

No. 19—"Hearts and Gizzards," an all-over pattern also called "Pierrot's Pom-Pom."

No. 20—"Japanese Lantern."

No. 21—"Silver and Gold," also "Star-of-the-East."

No. 22—"Mill Wheel."

No. 23—"Honeycomb."

No. 24—"Blindman's Fancy.

PLATE XVIII

In spite of their limited resources, the instinctive craving for the beautiful was the dominant incentive inspiring the brave hearts and industrious hands of the quilt-makers of the early nineteenth century, and aren't we of today fascinated with the primitive designs, the quaint florals, the precise geometrics, and the versions of local nomenclature that represented the occupations of their every-day life?

PLATE XVIII

No. 1—"Wheel of Mysterie," a fascinating patch, and even the most experienced quilter must beware, for it is all that the name implies. This is an all-over pattern and any combination of colors may be used but one should be much darker than the other, a decided contrast, then your quilt will be, "a thing of beauty and a joy forever." In some localities this pattern is called "Winding Ways."

No. 2—"Setting Sun." This patch was copied from a beautiful old quilt in the Thayer Museum—it was of hand-woven, hand-dyed cotton in red and white.

No. 3—"Rolling Pin-Wheel."

No. 4—"Double T."

No. 5—"Ferris Wheel" is an old pattern with a new name which recalls the World's Fair at Chicago in 1893. The originator of this pattern copied it from the oilcloth on her kitchen table many years ago, and called it "Hexagon." It is an all-over pattern and makes a very pleasing quilt.

Nos. 6 and 12—"Pin-Wheels." Two of the many designs called by this name.

No. 7—"Mixed T."

No. 8—"Wheel of Chance," also called "True Lovers' Buggy Wheel."

No. 9—"Brown Goose," also called "Double Z" an all-over pattern which reminds one of the funny old song grandmother sang when she rocked the children to sleep:

Go tell Aunt Rhoda, go tell Aunt Rhoda,
Go tell Aunt Rhoda her old brown goose is dead.

No. 10—"Double Z."

No. 11—"Turnabout T."

No. 13—"Wheel" or "Single Wedding Ring" in early nineteenth century.

No. 14—"Rainbow Tile," also "Diamond Field."

No. 15—"Capital T."

No. 16—"Rainbow Tile," designed and executed in rainbow shades by a nine-year-old girl in 1875.

No. 17—"French Bouquet" or "Grandmother's Flower Garden." Listen in on any group of ardent quilt fans and you will hear frequent mention of this most popular pattern of the day and it is not hard to see why. It has endless possibilities in the way of color combinations, and also in the way the blocks may be set together. Another matter of pride is the number of small hexagons in the finished quilt, often many thousands. In Colonial days it was called "Mosaic" or "Honeycomb." (See Part II, Plates VII and LXVI.)

No. 18—"Boutonniere." Instead of the old "Hexagon" of nineteenth century fame or the newer "French Bouquet," a twentieth century revival, a clever quilter "invented" this pattern and named it. To quote her own words: "It seems a shame not to pass this on, as it makes such a lacy, pretty design, with the airy vines in green and the stars of the print. The centers of the print stars are of a plain color that harmonizes."

No. 19—"Honeymoon Cottage."

No. 20—"Peeny Pen's Cottage."

"Peeny Pen's house by the side of the road
Looked like a little round hoppity toad."

No. 21—"Old Homestead." The little houses displayed on this plate are quaint and their charm, if any, is sentimental rather than artistic. They are specially attractive for a child's bed.

PLATE XIX

Historical, geographical, botanical, and comical—names that sparkle with a hint of imagination—add much to the charm of the finished quilt. Light pieces and dark—that's what makes patchwork so interesting— and so like life.

PLATE XIX

No. 1—"Winged Square."

No. 2—"Strips and Squares."

No. 3—"Carpenter's Square."

No. 4—"Burnham Square."

No. 5—"Square and Compass."

No. 6—"Nonesuch," also "Love Ring." The illustration shows the center of the quilt and when finished it will be a succession of rings, increasing in size. To be effective there should be a sharp contrast in the two colors used.

No. 7—"Drunkard's Path" or "Rocky Road to Dublin" before 1849— then called "Rocky Road to California" or "Country Husband." In Salem, Ohio, it was called "Robbing Peter to Pay Paul." The design is easy enough to arrange once a start is made—and this is not a temperance lecture either. (See Part II, Plate XXXIX.)

No. 8—"Vine of Friendship."

Nos. 9 and 10—"Fool's Puzzle." Same name but different arrangement of squares.

No. 11—"Falling Timber."

No. 12—"Wonder-of-the-World."

No. 13—"Around the World."

No. 14—"Rob Peter to Pay Paul." The patches used in blocks Nos. 6 to 14 inclusive were all cut by the same pattern. The difference of design is due to the arrangement of color and patches.

No. 15—"Double Square."

No. 16—"London Square."

No. 17—"Courthouse Square." Very much like one of the "Album" group.

No. 18—"Wind-blown Square." Also "Balkan Puzzle." A sort of topsy-turvy pattern.

No. 19—"Union Square."

No. 20—"Square and a Half."

PLATE XX

Life is like a patchwork quilt
And each little patch is a day,
Some patches are rosy, happy and bright,
And some are dark and gray.

But each little patch as it's fitted in
And sewn to keep it together
Makes a finished block in this life of ours
Filled with sun, and with rainy weather.

So let me work on Life's patchwork quilt
Through the rainy days and the sun—
Trusting that when I have finished my block
The Master may say: "Well done."
                    ELIZABETH RYAN DECOURSEY.

PLATE XX

No. 1—"Flying Clouds" is the name of this patch in New England but in the Middle West it is known as "Four Frogs."

No. 2—"Sunburst." The sun-god is as important in patchwork lore as in the life of the early Egyptians, and there are as many variations of design.

No. 3—"Snow Crystals." The myriad shapes of the minute snow-flake when held under a microscope are the inspiration of this unique design, the base of which is the ever beautiful diamond. (See Part II, Plate C)

No. 4—"Weather Vane." This pattern dates back to the time when every barn had one on its roof tree, and great-grandmother watched to see which way the wind was blowing instead of listening to a scientific forecast on the radio.

No. 5—"Flying Dutchman." An all-over pattern.

No. 6—"Sky Rocket." A first cousin to the "Stars."

No. 7—"Album Patch." There are many different patterns known as "Album" or "Autograph" patches. Almost every quilter made one to suit her particular fancy.

No. 8—"California Star," one of the most intricate and beautiful of "Star" patterns—much piecing to one block but not many blocks to the finished quilt.

No. 9—"Wheel of Fortune" of Pennsylvania Dutch origin and in some localities called the "Buggy Wheel."

No. 10—"The Philippines," a modern name given to one of the old-time patterns.

No. 11—"Feather Star" with "Saw Tooth" border.

No. 12—"Florida Star" a new design, very dainty and suitable for using small scraps of print with solid color of same shade.

No. 13—"Madam X." Modern all-over pattern.

No. 14—"Church Steps," a variation of the old "Log Cabin" pattern.

PLATE XXI

Great-Grandma made a "friendship quilt"
Of scraps of calico.
Her neighbors gave small bits of cloth
From each new gown, and so
Great-Grandma fashioned deftly
A quilt of cheerful hues,
And sewed with tiny stitches
The pinks, and grays, and blues.

ELIZABETH CRAWFORD YATES.

PLATE XXI

No. 1—"Crossed Canoes."

No. 2—"Double Irish Chain," also called "Chained Five-patch" (see Part II, Plate XCIX)

No. 3—"Eight Hands Around." A dance figure familiar to Colonial days.

Nos. 4 and 5—"Saw Tooth." There are many variations of this old-time pattern.

No. 6—"Walk Around," an all-over pattern of real charm in the finished quilt.

No. 7—"Triple Irish Chain." The "Irish Chain" patterns were very popular with Colonial, as well as present-day quilters, and deservedly so, for the finished quilt is very beautiful and simple in construction.

No. 9—"Follow-the-Leader," a children's game.

No. 10—"Cupid's Arrowpoint," an all-over pattern a bit different from the usual patchwork, since the center patch is white and the interest is in the border around it—because of its name one naturally thinks of shades of pink, both in plain color and in print.

No. 11—"Double Monkey Wrench." Also called "Love Knot," "Hole-in-the-Barn-Door," "Puss-in-the-Corner," "Shoo-Fly," "Lincoln's Platform," and "Sherman's March."

No. 12—"Album Patch." The original idea of the Album quilt was a gift for a bride-to-be. A group of friends would get together and each would piece a block and embroider her name upon it.

No. 13—"Friendship Knot" or "Starry Crown."

No. 14—"Friendship Ring," "Dresden Plate," or "Aster."

No. 15—"Swing-in-the-Center," a figure of the Square Dance.

No. 16—"Autograph Patch." A first cousin to the "Album" group and brings to mind the "Autograph Book" that was so popular in the latter part of the nineteenth century.

No. 17—"Friendship Quilt," an all-over pattern; each small patch should be a gift from a friend.

No. 18—"Hands-all-Around," a dance figure familiar to old and young in the pioneer days in the Middle West.

No. 19—"Castle Wall."

No. 20—"Dusty Miller," a design of striking beauty and worthy of a more esthetic name.

Nos. 21 and 8—Two interpretations of the Indian symbol "Swastika." Also called "The Pure Symbol of Right Doctrine," "Heart's Seal," "Chinese 10,000 Perfections," "Favorite of the Peruvians," "The Battle Ax of Thor," "Mound Builders," "Catch-Me-if-You-Can," and "Wind-Power of the Osages." If you are charmed by a piece of Indian pottery or a blanket of Indian design you will enjoy making a quilt from either one of these designs, which go farther back than the American Indian for their origin. These were favorite motifs of the early Egyptians.

PLATE XXII

The sun has such a pretty quilt
Each night he goes to bed,
It's made of lavender and gold,
With great long stripes of red.

And bordered by the softest tints
Of all the shades of gray.
It's put together by the sky,
And quilted by the day.

LAURA COATES REED

PLATE XXII

No. 1—"Snowball." There are several different patterns called "Snowball," "Base Ball," or "Pullman Puzzle."

No. 2—"Lazy Daisy." This seems to have been a favorite name in early times. This particular pattern looks very much like "Cupid's Arrowpoint."

No. 3—"Sunflower," also "Indian Summer" and "Broken Circle," an all-over pattern of entrancing beauty. Four blocks sewed together shows a complete design.

Nos. 4 and 6—"Sunflower." Two very intricate and beautiful designs having the same name. Also called "Blazing Sun" or "Blazing Star." This design was a great favorite in the early part of the nineteenth century and was usually developed in brown and yellow, the natural sunflower shades.

No. 5—"Kansas Sunflower."

No. 7—"Triple Sunflower." All Kansas quilters are interested in the various "Sunflower" patches as it is the Kansas State Flower.

No. 8—"Wild Goose Chase," a product of Civil War days.

No. 9—"Primrose Path."

No. 10—"Melon Patch." An all-over pattern.

No. 11—"Lafayette Orange Peel," an all-over pattern. Nos. 10 and 11 are very similar, in fact, they could be cut by the same pattern. The difference in design depends entirely upon the arrangement of colors.

No. 12—"Prickly Pear."

No. 13—"Sage Bud." This must have originated in Arizona or New Mexico.

No. 14—"Birds-in-the-Air." An old, old all-over pattern which has been reproduced literally hundreds of times.

No. 15—"Tulip Lady-Fingers." Would be most effective set together with squares of print like the center patch.

No. 16—"Autumn Tints." An all-over pattern developed in brown, red, two shades of yellow and a red print.

No. 17—"Garden Maze." Early nineteenth century design also called "Sun Dial," "Tirzah's Treasure," and "Tangled Garter."

No. 18—"Pineapple." An all-over pattern also called "Maltese Cross." (see Part II, Plate LXXXVIII)

No. 19—"Strawberrie," also called "Kentucky Beauty."

PLATE XXIII

Quilt names having political significance show that the women as well as the men felt a keen interest in the affairs of their country, and appreciating the freedom from monarchial rule, developed a political consciousness that was to prove the ancestor of our present twentieth century woman's suffrage.

PLATE XXIII

No. 1—"Free Trade Patch."

No. 2—"Lincoln's Platform."

No. 3—"Nelson's Victory." An old Connecticut pattern.

No. 4—"Burgoyne Surrounded" of Revolutionary period. In 1850 it was called the "Wheel of Fortune" and in 1860 in northern Ohio it was called "The Road to California."

No. 5—"Madison's Patch." President Madison as well as his famous wife had a patch named in his honor.

No. 6—"Democratic Donkey." Modern.

No. 7—"Elephant." (Ararat)

No. 8—"White House Steps."

No. 9—"President's Quilt."

No. 10—"The Little Giant," (Stephen A. Douglass), also called "Heart's Desire."

Nos. 11 and 13—"Old Tippecanoe." Two patches cut by the same pattern. The different arrangement of colors gives an entirely different design.

No. 14—"Whig's Defeat." A very old pattern.

No. 15—"Fifty-Four-Forty-or-Fight."

PLATE XXIV

*The ever-westward movement of the pioneer settler had much to do
with the changing of quilt pattern names. They reflect history's trend.
In this plate, patterns of faded quilts that covered Revolutionary heroes
in '76, and modern varieties, resplendent with color, range side by side.*

PLATE XXIV

No. 1—"Philadelphia Pavement," a great favorite in old-time Pennsylvania.

No. 2—"Bridal Stairway," an all-over pattern forming a double
stairway effect across the quilt, and with a "Bouquet" or "Feather
Wreath" design quilted into the large squares it would make a beautiful
quilt.

No. 3—"State-of-Ohio."

No. 4—"The Reel," an old-time favorite very much like "Order
No. 11."

No. 5—"Shoo-Fly," a nine-patch variation closely related to "Duck
and Ducklings" and others.

No. 6—"Chimney Sweep." This is very much like some of the
"Album" group with the name omitted.

No. 7—"Mother's Dream."

No. 8—"Kansas Troubles," an all-over pattern.

No. 9—"Rose Dream." A patch that uses the summertime rose as
its motif would be a very cheery one to work on during the bleak
winter months. Its very name seems to promise sunshine and flowers.
This may account for its great popularity.

No. 10—"Golden Gate" or "Winged Square," a great favorite of the
pioneer bride-to-be.

No. 11—"Kansas Dugout," an all-over pattern of late nineteenth
century origin.

No. 12—"Double Wedding Ring." Real quilt enthusiasts delight in
this all-over pattern but it is hardly the design for the novice to undertake.

Nos. 13 and 14—"Lady-of-the-Lake" originated in Vermont in 1810.
Heroic tales of Sir Walter Scott were especially interesting to men and
women of pioneer instincts and the women honored the author in their
most practical form of artistic self-expression. This is one of the few
patterns which has never been known by any other name.

No. 15—"Square and Circle. Insignia of the Presidents and Past
Presidents' General Assembly. Colors red, purple, crimson, and white.

No. 16—"Texas Tears."

No. 17—"Double Pyramids." An all-over pattern from Virginia,
c. 1819.

No. 18—"Pieced Pyramids." A modern all-over pattern.

No. 19—"Odd Fellow's Patch."

PLATE XXV

Who fashioned first a patchwork tree
An emblem wrought, unconsciously:
God fashioned trees for mankind's good—
Man straightway hewed a Cross of wood.

MINNIE M. ROBERTSON

PLATE XXV

No. 1—"Bay Leaf," also "Tea Leaves." An all-over pattern.

No. 2—"Pine Tree." Modern.

No. 3—"Iris Leaf," also "Wandering Foot."

No. 4—"Sweet Gum Leaf."

No. 5—"Tea Leaf."

No. 6—"English Ivy." Seldom does any one, even the most zealous quilt connoisseur, see a finer example of the art of quilt-making than was the original of this unique pattern. The colors, home-dyed evidently, for the quilt was over a hundred years old, were a deep rich rose and a meadow green.

No. 7—"Forbidden-Fruit Tree."

No. 8—"Pine Tree," also "Temperance Tree." One of the very oldest of Colonial patterns. In all its migrations from coast to coast, it did not change its name, and will remain one of the most beautiful of all "Tree" patterns. Many variations of this pattern have been given other names.

No. 9—"Tall Pine Tree." An all-over pattern. Modern.

No. 10—"Shamrock."

No. 11—"Little Beech Tree."

No. 12—"Live-Oak Tree."

No. 13—"Tree-of-Temptation." Note the branches hang very low and the flowers are within easy reach.

No. 14—"Hozanna" or "The Palm," a patch of pre-Revolutionary origin in Maine. The religious significance of this patch is very apparent and it was designed by one with true artistic instinct, for had the heavy parts of all four sections been turned toward the center of the block the artistic proportions would have been lost. This is an all-over pattern and in setting the blocks together this arrangement should be carried out all over the quilt.

No. 15—"Formosa Tea Leaf."

No. 16—"Autumn Leaf" or "Maple Leaf."

Nos. 17 and 18—"Tree-of-Paradise." Two very beautiful designs of Massachusetts origin, and not so very unlike.

No. 19—"Christmas Tree," also "Tree of Life." (see Part II, Plate XXVII)

PLATE XXVI

Roses red and violets blue
And all the sweetest flowers that in the forest grew.
                                            SPENCER

PLATE XXVI

No. 1—"White Rose." An all-over pattern.

No. 2—"Daisy Chain." An all-over pattern. White petals and yellow centers on a green hexagon.

No. 3—"Meadow Daisy" or "Black-eyed Susan."

No. 4—"Modernistic Trumpet Vine." Pieced.

No. 5—"Modernistic Pansy." Pieced.

No. 6—"Spice Pink." Very old.

No. 7—"Scotch Thistle."

No. 8—"Daisy Applique." An all-over pattern. When four patches are sewed together they form a complete flower.

No. 9—"Mountain Pink."

Nos. 10, 11, 12, and 13—"Four different interpretations of the "Poinsettia" or "Flower of Christmas.""

No. 14—"Friendship Dahlia."

PLATE XXVII

Flowers, Plants and Fishes
Beasts, Birds, Flyes and Bees
Hills, Dales, Plains, Pastures
Skies, Seas, Rivers, Trees,
There's nothing near at hand or farthest sought
But with the needle may be wrought.

From an old sampler.

PLATE XXVII

No. 1—"Tassel Plant."

No. 2—"Morning-glories." Modern.

No. 3—"Rose Bud."

No. 4—"English Flower Pot." Modern.

No. 5—"Bleeding Heart."

No. 6—Maude Hare's "Flower Garden."

No. 7—"Cornucopia." Modern.

No. 8—"Old-Fashioned Nosegay." Note the lace paper holder.

No. 9—"Modernistic California Poppy." Pieced. All-over design.

No. 10—"Crimson Rambler," also "Spring Beauty." The crimson rambler has ever been a favorite flower and this may account for the popularity of this pattern.

No. 11—"English Poppy." Very old and very crude.

No. 12—"Autumn Flowers," original design by Carrie A. Hall.

No. 13—"Old-Fashioned Flower Garden."

No. 14—"Love Apple." (See Part II, Plate V.) The Love Apple or Tomato was thought to be poisonous and not fit to eat prior to 1850. The plants were grown for ornament in the flower gardens of many homes. Today it is one of our most delicious vegetables.

No. 15—"Cherry." All-over pattern.

No. 16—"Horn of Plenty," original design by Carrie A. Hall. Applique, unlike pieced patches, offers opportunity for diversifications and embellishments, the designs may be just as elaborate as the maker chooses, and her originality has more chance to assert itself.

PLATE XXVIII

GRANDMA'S QUILT
With gentle and loving fingers
She caressed the well worn fold;
'Round each piece a mem'ry lingers
Like a sweet story often told.

SYLVIA SUMMERS PIERCE

PLATE XXVIII

No. 1—"Lady-Fingers and Sunflowers."

No. 2—"Double Peony and Wild Rose."

No. 3—"Mexican Rose."

No. 4—"Ohio Rose." (see Part II, Plate CII)

No. 5—"Mountain Laurel," c. 1820.

No. 6—"Wind-Blown Rose." Modern.

No. 7—"Golden Corn."

No. 8—"Pineapple." Original quilt in Thayer Museum.

No. 9—"English Rose."

No. 10—"Conventional Rose." Indiana, c. 1840.

PLATE XXIX

Far and near I sought
Utterance in a thought
A garden ever blooming, just for you;

So flowers that will not wilt
I stitched into a quilt,
My treasure-trove of memories for you.
                              JOSEPHINE DAY MICKLESON

PLATE XXIX

No. 1—"Four Peonies." Very old design.

No. 2—"Peonies." Very old design, c. 1820. Prize quilt of the Middle West.

No. 3—"Peony Patch." In Colonial times it was called "Piney."

No. 4—"Peony." Star of LeMoyne design.

No. 5—"Double Peony."

No. 6—"Aunt Martha's Wild Rose." Modern.

No. 7—"Old-Fashioned Rose." Mountain Mist design.

No. 8—"Rose of Sharon." (see Part II, Plate XLIX)

No. 9—"Pomegranite."

No. 10—"Topeka Rose." Named in honor of the B. P. W. Club of Topeka.

No. 11—"Mrs. Harris' Colonial Rose."

No. 12—"Sadie's Choice Rose." Very old pattern.

PLATE XXX

I am the Rose of Sharon
And the lily of the valleys.
As the lily among the thorns
So is my love among the daughters;
As the apple tree among the trees of the wood
So is my beloved among the sons.

Songs of Solomon.

PLATE XXX

No. 1—"Original Rose," made in 1840.

No. 2—"Original Rose No. 3." Made in Indiana, c. 1855.

No. 3—Earliest known "Rose of Sharon."

No. 4—"Rose of Sharon." c. 1865.

No. 5—"Rose of Sharon." c. 1850.

No. 6—"Rose of Sharon." Another interpretation. (For still another interpretation see Plate XXIX, No. 8)

No. 7—"Rose of Sharon," made in Pennsylvania c. 1840. The flowers are very crude. Small diamonds are used as leaves, and no attempt is made to conform to the natural leaf-shape.

No. 8—"Rose of Sharon." Very old but more graceful than many others.

No. 9—"Rose of Sharon." Twentieth century interpretation.

No design has more variations than this same romantic "Rose of Sharon"—all are of the built-up rose flower with leaves, buds, and stems, but arrangements vary in varying localities and almost all are lovely.

PLATE XXXI

PIONEER QUILTERS

With busy fingers but with voices gay,
They quilted treasure troves for you and me.
No time for idle thoughts, then, thrifty souls,
Their quilts would live in pictured history.

IRENE F. COHEN

PLATE XXXI

No. 1—"The Rose of LeMoyne," of French inspiration but distinctively Colonial-American.   (See Plate III, No. 1.)

No. 2—"Whig Rose."

No. 3—"Whig Rose." In Pennsylvania in 1845 it was called the "Democrat Rose." Both parties claimed it and the dispute never was settled. (see Part II, Plate LXXXIII)—an entirely different design called "Democrat Rose."

No. 4—"Rose Tree," adapted from a rare old quilt from Switzerland.

No. 5—"Combination Rose," c. 1850, also called "California Rose," and when it is developed in yellow it is called "Texas Yellow Rose."

No. 6—"Rose Applique," a simple design often used for first lessons in the art of needlework.

No. 7—"Missouri Rose" (See Part II, Plate XIV), also called the "Rose Tree" and "Prairie Flower."

No. 8—"Virginia Rose." Original design by Caroline Stalnaker of West Virginia, c. 1855.

No. 9—"Harrison Rose," c. 1840. This is a combined effect of piecing and applique.

No. 10—"Wild Rose." Twentieth century design.

No. 11—"Rose Cross," one of the most popular of antique patterns. This pattern shows a decorative combination of a cross motif and a foundation rose pattern. (See Part II, Plate XXXII.)

PLATE XXXII

Curiously wrought in stitches, line on line,
Faded, yet fair, these ancient calicoes
Bespeak the patient work of one who knows
No weariness in finish or design.

AMY SMITH.

PLATE XXXII

No. 1—"Modernistic Rose." Pieced.

Nos. 2 and 10—"Ohio Rose.   c. 1850.

No. 3—"Indiana Rose."

No. 4—"Loretta's Rose."   Named in honor of Mrs. Loretta Selover, President of the Kansas Federation of B. P. W. C.

No. 5—"Conventional Wild Rose."

No. 6—"Wild Rose."

Nos. 7 and 8—"Mexican Rose," c. 1842.   Note the diamond shaped leaves in No. 8 and the very crudely shaped flower.

No. 9—"Mrs. Kretsinger's Rose."   This is the original "Whig Rose." (See Part II, Plate LXXV.)

No. 11—"Radical Rose."   After the second year of the Civil War, talk of radicals and radicalism was heard on all occasions and a famous quilt-maker put a black center in the patch she was making and called it a "Radical Rose."   Inasmuch as the freeing of the slaves was the cause of more than half the trouble she thought it was only fair that they should be represented in some way, so after that she put a black center in all her "Radical Rose" patches.

PLATE XXXIII

Among my treasure trove is a patch quilt whose red flowers spring-ing from small green leaves delighted the eye that saw it in the brown-walled log cabin. "Hit hasn't got any right name," I was told. "I call hit the mountain lily. I just drew it off from these here mountain lilies that bloom along in July." . . . I have always hated people who called whatever they admired "a poem" but that was the word that came to me while this mountain woman told me how her mind had seized and her hands made captive the beauty of the mountain lily, in the one form of expression that was her own.

ELIZABETH DANGERFIELD in *Patchwork Quilts and Philosophy.*

PLATE XXXIII

No. 1—"Lily" pattern based on the LeMoyne Star.

No. 2—"Lily-of-the-Valley."

No. 3—"North Carolina Lily." In Tennessee and Kentucky this was called "Mountain Lily"; in Ohio and Illinois the "Fire Lily"; in the Middle West the "Prairie Lily" or the "Noon-Day Lily"; in New England the "Wood Lily"; in Connecticut the "Meadow Lily"; and in California the "Mariposa Lily." This is a lovely design suggestive of old plantation life, with its atmosphere of quiet and leisure which afforded time for even so intricate a pattern as this. The only difference between Lily and Tulip designs of this type is that the lily is usually smaller and the tulip larger and more colorful. (See Part II, Plate XXXI.)

No. 4—"Water Lily."

No. 5—"Water Lily." An all-over pattern. Four patches sewed together form the design. White flowers with yellow centers on a pale green background.

No. 6—"Easter Lily." Original design by Harold Fisher. White flowers with small edging of pale green and darker green leaves on a pale blue background.

No. 7—"Modernistic Acorn." Pieced.

No. 8—"Lily of the Field." Of religious significance.

No. 9—"Tobacco Leaf." Probably of Virginia origin but often found among New England patterns.

No. 10—"Acorn and Oak Leaf." Mountain Mist design.

No. 11—"Tiger Lily." Pennsylvania Dutch design, c. 1837.

No. 12—"Tulip-Tree Leaves." A favorite of the mountain women of South Carolina.

No. 13—"Hero's Crown."

No. 14—"Hickory Leaf" or "Order No. 11." Authoritatively known as the "Hickory Leaf." The story is thus: Fannie Kreeger Haller, a ten-year-old girl, saw her mother's choice new quilt snatched from their bed by marauders when "Order No. 11" was the issue—she carried the treasured design in her mind and years after reproduced the quilt, christening it "Order No. 11." This story is vouched for by Mrs. Roxie Soper, who was a personal friend of Mrs. Haller's daughter. George C. Bingham, a noted painter of Arrow Rock, Missouri, now of Independence, made this scene immortal in his picture "Martial Law or Order No. 11." Recently the State of Missouri has created a State Park at Arrow Rock; it includes "Big Spring," the house that was used for the first "Young Ladies' School" in Missouri; also "Old Tavern," and the home of General George C. Bingham.

No. 15—"Oak Leaf and Acorn."

No. 16—"Oak Leaf." A New England pattern. (See Part II, Plate XXIII.)

No. 17—"Charter Oak."

No. 18—"Oak Leaf and Cherries."

No. 19—"Pride-of-the-Forest."

PLATE XXXIV

A pure raindrop and a brave sunbeam
From a rainbow eloped one day;
And their children, Iris by man named,
Now make our gardens gay.

'Tis true their season of bloom is short,
But fingers patient and deft
Have in this quilt their tints preserved,
And a lasting tribute left.

EMMA UPTON VAUGHN.

PLATE XXXIV

Nos. 1, 3, and 4—These are different interpretations of the beautiful "Iris Applique."

No. 2—"Modernistic Iris." Pieced.

No. 5—"Vase of Autumn Leaves." Original design by Carrie A. Hall.

No. 6—"Texas Flower"; also "Texas Treasure."

No. 7—"Nose-Gay." Modern.

No. 8—"Fleur-de-Lis." An authentic old design. The motif is often used as a basis for quilting designs.

Nos. 9 and 10—"Pineapple." The same name for two entirely different old-time designs.

No. 11—"Hyacinths."

No. 12—"Magnolia Bud." A modernistic pattern bringing a promise of spring.

No. 13—"Wind-Blown Tulips."

Nos. 14 and 15—"Lotus Bud" and "Lotus Flower." Egyptian in inspiration—highly prized designs used alternately in the same quilt.

No. 16—"Coxcomb."

No. 17—"Currants and Coxcomb." Prize design.

No. 18—"Pine Burr."

No. 19—"The Urn." Designed and made in 1848 by a child seven years old. The original quilt is in the Thayer Museum. Time has mellowed the old-fashioned reds and greens and yellow print set on a once white background.

PLATE XXXV

Restive and unconquered are the little seas
That Holland from her green bowl fills
With wine of Tulips.

PLATE XXXV

No. 1—"Full Blown Tulip." Pennsylvania Dutch c. 1835.   A very intricate design.

No. 2—"Anna's Irish Tulip."   Modern.

No. 3—"Tulips in Vase"; also "Royal Japanese Vase."

No. 4—"Tulip Garden."

No. 5—"Four Tulips."

No. 6—"Tulip Applique."

No. 7—"Grandma's Tulips."

No. 8—"Cottage Tulips." (See Part II, Plate XCIV), called "Texas Star."

No. 9—"Dutch Tulip."

No. 10—"Anna Bauersfeld's Tulip."

No. 11—"Mrs. Ewer's Tulip."   Very old pattern.

No. 12—"Tulip."   Modern interpretation.

No. 13—"Old Dutch Tulip."   Original design by Carrie A. Hall.

No. 14—"Modernistic Tulip."   Pieced.

No. 15—"Conventional Tulip."   Ohio, c. 1840.

No. 16—"Colonial Tulip."   Very old pattern.

No. 17—"Cleveland Tulip."

PLATE XXXVI

I loved the Wreath of Roses, the Rose of Sharon, too—
But Grandmother's favorite was the True Lover's Knot in blue.
                                    CARLIE SEXTON.

The wreath was a design of never-failing delight. Both colonial and modern quilt-makers have used it with satisfactory results. The wreath motif, varied in detail according to the whim of the maker, might be any kind or combination of flowers.

PLATE XXXVI

No. 1—"Wreath of Carnations." Very old pattern with a modern name.

No. 2—"Feather Crown" with a "Ragged Robin" in center.

No. 3—"Hollyhock Wreath." Very old—note the diamond-shaped leaves.

No. 4—"President's Wreath." Early Colonial.

No. 5—"Wreath of Roses"; also "Garden Wreath."

No. 6—"Wreath of Wild Roses." Modern.

No. 7—"Wreath of Pansies."

No. 8—"Martha Washington's Wreath," c. 1820.

No. 9—"Iowa Rose Wreath."

No. 10—"Ben Hur's Chariot Wheel"; also "Princess Feather," from an Indiana family of French-Swiss ancestry.

No. 11—"Princess Feather." This name has reference to the plumes worn by the Knights and their Ladies. Also called "Star and Plumes."

PLATE XXXVII

You seem to spell romance, dear old quilts of mine
And my thoughts love to dwell on that happy olden time
When deft fingers fashioned flowers, leaves, and baskets, too—
Each year that you are with me I grow more fond of you.
CARLIE SEXTON.

Baskets—new ones, old ones, perfectly gorgeous ones, absolutely original ones—all a joy to behold. Baskets have always been a favorite pattern and there are many varieties from the simple pieced ones to the more elaborate appliqued flower baskets and most of them are of New England origin.

PLATE XXXVII

No. 1—"Cake Stand."

No. 2—"Basket-of Daisies."

No. 3—"Grandmother's Basket" is one of the very old designs which is still popular.

No. 4—"Basket-of-Oranges."

No. 5—"Mrs. Hall's Basket."

No. 6—"Bread Basket."

No. 7—"Basket of Flowers."

No. 8—"Maude Hare's Basket."

No. 9—"Carlie Sexton's Flower Basket."

No. 10—"Four Little Baskets."

Nos. 11 and 13—"Basket of Lilies" or "Basket of Tulips," Philadelphia, 1839.

No. 12—"Grape Basket."

No. 14—"Cherry Basket."

No. 15—"Cactus Basket" or "Desert Rose."

No. 16—"Tiny Basket."

Nos. 17 and 19—"Flower Pot." Two similar designs of the same name.

No. 18—"Colonial Basket."

Part 2

Quilts of Colonial Ancestry and of
Modern Design

THIS quilt was made by Mrs. Nellis, a pioneer of Topeka, Kansas, and is now the cherished possession of the "Woman's Club." It is a map of Kansas. The counties are represented by colored patches of silks and velvets, the edges being held together by embroidery stitches after the manner of the crazy quilt that was so popular in the latter part of the nineteenth century. The county seats are represented by a star, the rivers are outlined with chenille thread, and the railroads are marked by a line of gold thread. The border is of light brown satin upon which are embroidered numerous sunflowers—the state flower—also the name "KANSAS" and the date of admission to the Union, 1861, and the date the quilt was made, 1885. The state seal at the top is hand painted.

Kansas! Fair State, we well may claim
A meed of praise for thee;
None other boasts so great a fame,
So grand a history,
As through oppressions, strifes and wars
She soars triumphant to the stars."

—*Margaret Kilmer.*

MY MOTHER'S QUILTS

Within our sitting room a table stood,
Made by my father out of cherry wood,
On which thru summer day and winter night
A basket rested full of patches bright;
And from those scraps of variegated shade
My mother planned the many quilts she made,
From muslin and cretonne by some deft spell
Forming the flowers she loved so well;
The crimson tulip and the wild rose, too,
Were fashioned, each in its own shape and hue;
The drooping lily bent its modest head,
The pink carnations' perfume seemed to shed.

Oft from the brass-bound chests her quilts I take,
And from their folds the scented herb leaves shake;
Then on her own great, square four-post bed
The cunning labor of her hands I spread;
With lingering caress I softly touch
The beauty, oddly quaint, she prized so much,
While memory brings back the homely room
Where those bright blocks of flowers flamed in bloom.

Now for long years her patient toil is o'er;
Her quilt hands create her dreams no more;
Beneath a quilt of pinks and lilies too—
The prototypes from which her patterns grew—
She rests in peace. There, while she calmly sleeps,
God's mystic coverlet above her creeps.

This be my faith: That some day I shall see
Life's complex pattern growing plain to me;
That somewhere I shall clearly understand
The great design worked by the Master's hand;
And that somehow love's thread may reunite
Our broken lives into a fabric bright,
And in celestial arabesques restore
The ties that bind us here on earth no more.
                              CARRIE O'NEAL.

PLATE I

Courtesy of Mrs. M. E. Thorpe

GLAZED CHINTZ QUILT
Made in the town of Feathered, County Cork, Ireland, in 1680,
showing the type of quilt in use in other countries before the
colonists devised the pieced quilt.

PLATE II   *Collection of* ***Fern Bauersfeld***

OLD WOOLEN CRAZY QUILT
This quilt has been in constant use since 1850. The kind of
quilt that kept our colonial ancestors from having pneumonia.

PLATE III   *Collection of Fern Bauersfeld*

TEA ROSE

Colonial quilt made in Ohio in 1828 (see "Old Fashioned Quilts"
by Carlie Sexton). This copy made in Ohio in 1850. Note the
white spots in the flowers caused by the colored design wearing
out, showing the cotton filling.

PLATE IV *Collection of Fern Bauersfeld*

LUCINDA'S STAR
This quilt made by owner's great-grandmother in 1850 in Ohio.
Colors: red, blue, and deep yellow.

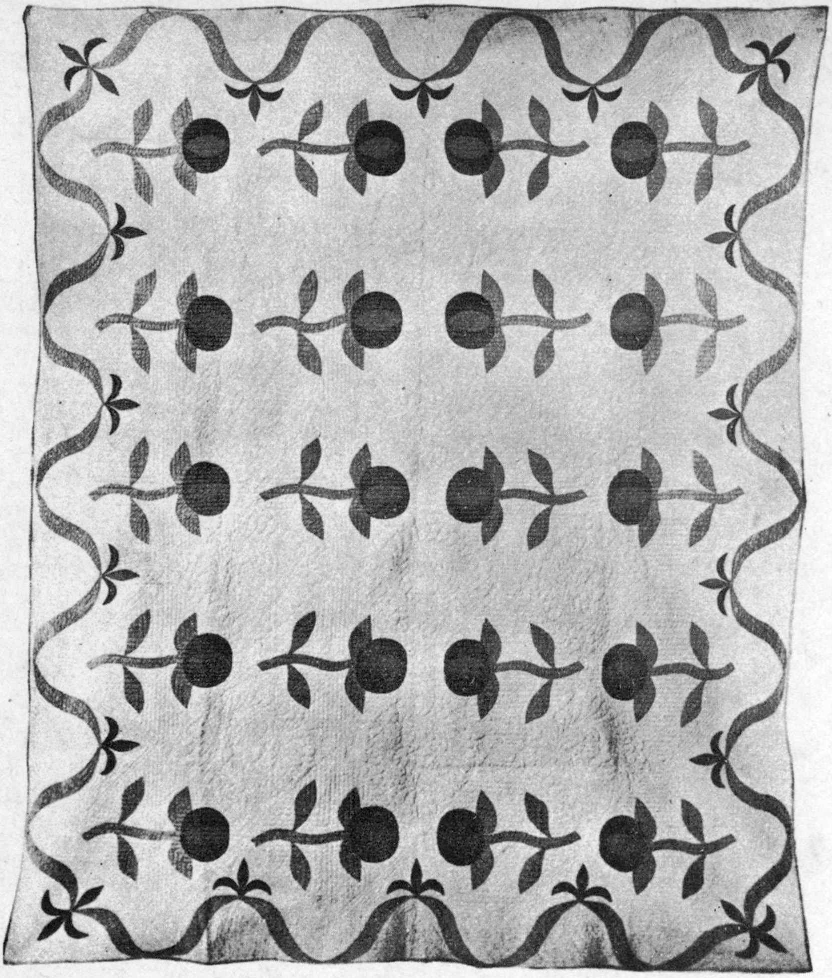

PLATE V   *Collection of Fern Bauersfeld*

LOVE APPLE
Made by owner's great-grandmother in 1850, in Ohio. A very
fine example of early quilt-making.

PLATE VI   *Courtesy of Mrs. P. W. Darrah*

CROSSES AND LOSSES
An unusual effect in blue and white with beautiful quilting.

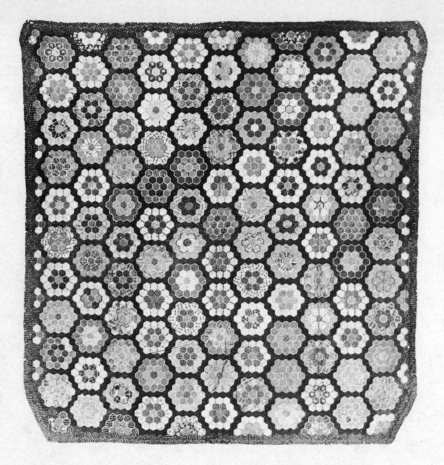

PLATE VII   *Courtesy of Mrs. Frances Larimer*

MOSAIC

Mosaic quilt of worsted. Dividing lines are of black, and all
seams are finished with a fine feather stitching. Made by
Frances Morton, mother of the present owner, in 1885. This
quilt could be termed the "Grandmother" of Grandmother's
Flower Gardens" which are so popular with present-day
quilters.

THE PATCHWORK QUILT

Of all the things a woman's hands have made,
The quilt so lightly thrown across her bed—
The quilt that keeps her loved ones warm—
Is woven of her love and dreams and thread.

When I have spoken to you of its beauty—
"A mere hodge-podge of calico," you said,
"A necessity of homely fashioning,
Just a covering made of cloth and thread."

I knew you'd missed the message hidden there
By hands that fashioned quilts so long ago.
Ambition and assurance are the patches
And the stitches of a quilt are love, I know.

I think a quilt is something very real—
A message of creation wrought in flame;
With grief and laughter sewn into its patches
I see beyond the shadows, dream and aim.

CARRIE A. HALL.

PLATE VIII   *Courtesy of Wolfe Studio*

LONE STAR
Interesting border arrangement and quilting. Note the date
1929 quilted in the white band between the borders.

PLATE IX   *Courtesy of Edna Mae Martin*

LONE STAR
This quilt was made by owner's mother in 1910. Colors red and
white with interesting quilting design.

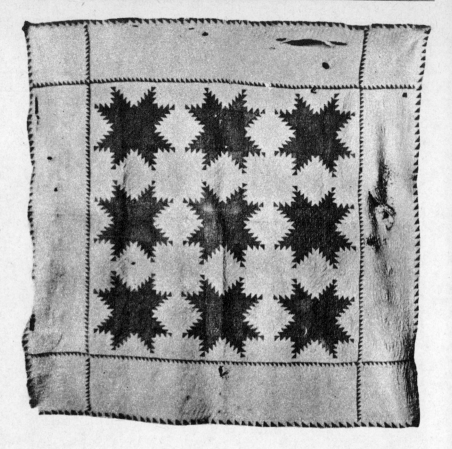

PLATE X   *Courtesy of Mrs. Helen Kinnett*

FEATHER STAR

Made in 1771 by the great-great-grandmother of the present
owner, Helen Kinnett, who said: "It was given to my great-
grandmother, Helen Jackson, when she was twelve years old;
then to my grandmother, who was the second Helen; then to my
mother, who was the third Helen; she gave it to my Aunt Helen
Goens, who died leaving it to me, I being the fifth Helen."

PLATE XI   *Courtesy of Mary Ellen Everhard*

FEATHER STAR
An old family heirloom made by Mrs. Jane Duguid on a Virginia plantation in 1858. The material is blue and yellow figured print with muslin, with a very interesting border effect and quilting design. Mrs. Duguid was the grandmother of the present owner.

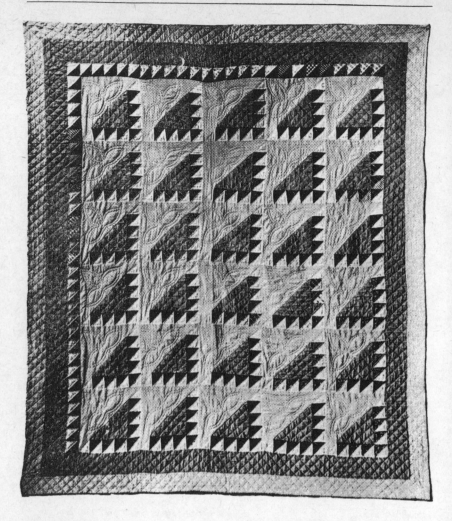

PLATE XII   *Courtesy of Mrs. Harrison Putney*

SAW TOOTH
This pattern is also called "Lend and Borrow," "Rocky Glen,"
and "Indian Meadow."   A very interesting old quilt.

PLATE XIII   *Courtesy of Mrs. Fred Keller*

DOUBLE SAW TOOTH
Made by Mrs. Anna Bueneman in 1874 and given to the present
owner.

PLATE XIV   *Courtesy of Lora Cheseldene*

THE ROSE TREE
Also called "Missouri Rose," made by owner's grandmother,
Mrs. Lucinda Chesnut, in 1845. (See Plate CIX.)

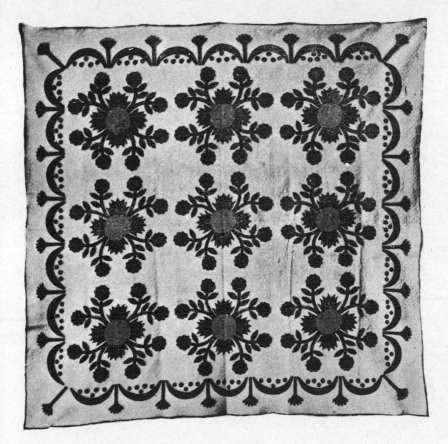

PLATE XV   *Courtesy of Mrs. Charles Blankenstine*

ROSE OF SHARON
Made by Mrs. Elizabeth Donly of West Alexandria, Pennsylvania, for her son, Clement, who was Mrs. Blankenstine's father.

PLATE XVI   *Courtesy of Mrs. Grace Potter*

ROSE APPLIQUE
Made by owner in 1930. Note the beautiful quilting and interesting border.

PLATE XVII   *Courtesy of Mrs. Grace Potter*

WREATH OF ROSES
Made by owner's mother, Susan B. Klaus, when she was sixteen years old, 1860. Note the interesting manner of setting
the patches together.

PLATE XVIII   *Courtesy of Mrs. C. W. Chase*

FENCE RAIL
Made by Mrs. Chase of Mobile, Alabama, in 1901 for a Christmas gift to her mother, Mrs. J. C. Lysle, who left it to her granddaughter, May Chase Wickersham. The quilt is a "family tree"; each of the thirty-five blocks represents one branch of the family, with names of the parents embroidered on the black strip and names of the children on the colored strips. The patches are of silk and all from the "family scrap bag," many of them being of wedding dresses. The lining is of brown broche taffeta and was the skirt of Mrs. Lysle's wedding dress in 1861.

PLATE XIX   *Collection of Mrs. W. A. Jeffers*

BLAZING STAR

Made by the owner's mother, Mrs. J. C. Lysle, in 1890. The large star is of various colored diamonds with tips of star and center star in red, as are the small stars and border. It is an exact copy of an heirloom made in Mount Vernon, Pennsylvania, in 1800.

PLATE XX   *Collection of Mrs. W. A. Jeffers*

STUFFED SILK QUILT

Made by Mrs. Edmonds in 1880. It is stuffed with wool sheared
from sheep of her father's flock. Edge is finished with a ruffle
of same material as the lining.

PLATE XXI   *Collection of Mrs. W. A. Jeffers*

SAW TOOTH

A most interesting design in orange and figured green print.
Made in 1920. The quilting of this unusual quilt is very beautiful.

PLATE XXII   *Collection of Mrs. W. A. Jeffers*

INDIANA PUZZLE

A very old pattern reproduced in rose and white in a modern
quilt. Made in 1920.

OAK LEAF

This is a most effective combination of dark blue print and white—the quilting was especially designed to fit the spaces.

PLATE XXIV *Collection of Mrs. W. A. Jeffers*

ROSE APPLIQUE
This quilt was made from a Webster pattern in 1922. Colors are several shades of pink and green.

PLATE XXV   *Collection of Mrs. W. A. Jeffers*

POPPY
Copied from a Webster pattern in 1922. The colors used are
true to nature and the quilt is very beautiful.

PLATE XXVI

BOUQUET OF GARDEN FLOWERS

This beautiful specimen of quilt-craft was made entirely by hand by Emma Ann Covert of Lebanon, Ohio, about 1842. A small figured print of green is used for the leaves, stems, small baskets, and bases of the large baskets, with red print for the flowers, buds, and large baskets. The design is appliqued on a fine homespun with a reversed buttonhole stitch and the quilting is done in the grape pattern. The owner of this valued heirloom is a granddaughter of the maker.

PLATE XXVII   *Courtesy of Mrs. W. C. Harris*

ROSE APPLIQUE AND TREE OF LIFE
Reproductions of two very old colonial patterns.

PLATE XXVIII   *Courtesy of Mrs. Charles Biggler*

FLOWER POTS
This is a reproduction of an old quilt over one hundred years old.

PLATE XXIX   *Courtesy of Mrs. Charles Biggler*

RAINBOW STAR

Made entirely of printed scraps and the color effect is very
beautiful. There are eight thousand tiny diamond patches in
the stars and border.

PLATE XXX   *Courtesy of Major Sterling A. Wood, U.S.A.*

SILK CRAZY QUILT

Made by Mrs. Kate Richardson and her daughter, Ida May—
grandmother and mother of Major Wood, at Tuscaloosa, Alabama, in 1883. The variety of embroidered and hand-painted
designs make this a very beautiful specimen of the popular
quilt of that period. (See Plate LXXI and Plate XCII.)

A CRAZY QUILT

They do not make them any more,
For quilts are cheaper at the store
Than woman's labor, though a wife
Men think the cheapest thing in life.
But now and then a quilt is spread
Upon a quaint old walnut bed,
A crazy quilt of those old days
That I am old enough to praise.

Some woman sewed these points and squares
Into a pattern like life's cares.
Here is a velvet that was strong,
The poplin that she wore so long,
A fragment from her daughter's dress,
Like her, a vanished loveliness;
Old patches of such things as these,
Old garments and old memories.

And what is life?   A crazy quilt;
Sorrow and joy, and grace and guilt,
With here and there a square of blue
For some old happiness we knew;
And so the hand of time will take
The fragments of our lives and make,
Out of life's remnants, as they fall,
A thing of beauty, after all.

DOUGLAS MALLOCH.

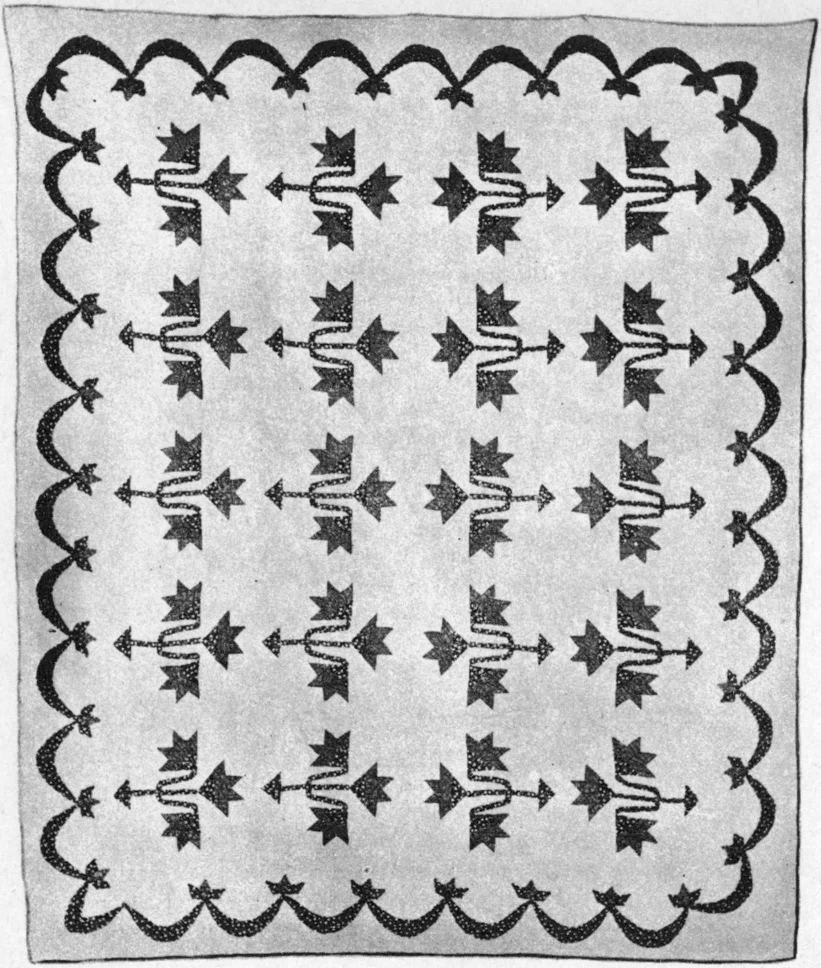

PLATE XXXI   *Courtesy of Virginia Green Holloway*

NORTH CAROLINA LILY

A very fine example of this antique pattern and unusual in that
the leaves, stems, and border are of a black and white print instead of the usual green.

ROSE CROSS
Modern quilt of Colonial inspiration made in 1931. The quilting is lovely.

PLATE XXXIII   *Courtesy of Mrs. C. W. Shreve*

GRAPE VINE

An original design of grape vine border with motifs of garden
flowers. Made by Mrs. Ann Coates Shreve in 1855. The grape
leaves are of green print, the vines of a dull brown print, the
grapes of a purple print, and stuffed. The flowers and the
basket are also stuffed. This is a most beautiful picture in
fabric handiwork, perfect in design and workmanship, and needs
to be seen to be appreciated.

PLATE XXXIV   *Courtesy of Mrs. Augusta Wehrman*

STRAWBERRY QUILT
This quilt was made in 1875, and was a wedding gift to Mrs.
Wehrman from her mother-in-law. Colors: red, orange, and
green. The colors are somewhat faded but because of the unusual design it is a valued heirloom.

PLATE XXXV   *Courtesy of Mrs. C. E. Van Vleck*

MAGIC VINE

This quilt was made by the owner, and took first prize in a
contest sponsored by the *Topeka Daily Capital*. Contest was
based on quality of needlework, quilting, and general artistic
effect obtained by the blending of colors.

PLATE XXXVI   *Courtesy of Mrs. C. E. Van Vleck*

BASKET OF SUNFLOWERS
An original design by the owner. Very modern and a quilt of
exceptionally beautiful handicraft.

MOSS ROSE APPLIQUE

Made by Mrs. Susan B. Stayman in 1853. The design is original and took first prize at the Galesburg, Illinois, Fair in 1855. The colors are as bright as when new.

PLATE XXXVIII   *Collection of Mary M. Stayman*

DAHLIA WREATH
Made by Mrs. Susan B. Stayman in 1855. An original design
with an interesting border.

PLATE XXXIX   *Collection of Mary M. Stayman*

DRUNKARD'S PATH
Made by owner in 1930. A very old pattern made of dark green
print and white, with special quilting designs.

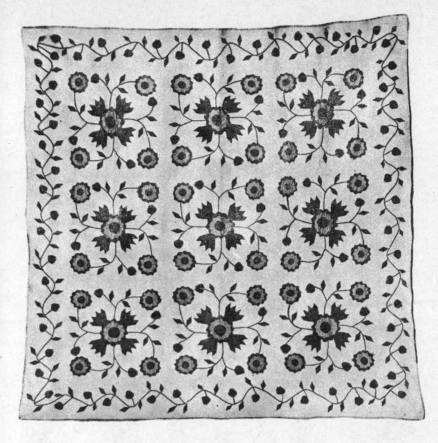

PLATE XL   *Collection of Dora Spencer Holman*

CALIFORNIA ROSE
Made by Jane Ewalt, Paris, Kentucky, 1850, at age of seventeen years. Mrs. Holman is a granddaughter.

PLATE XLI   *Collection of Dora Spencer Holman*

RISING SUN
Made by owner's mother, Mrs. D. D. Spencer, in Leavenworth,
1917. Note the variety of quilting designs.

PLATE XLII   *Collection of Dora Spencer Holman*

TULIP QUILT
Made by owner's mother, Mrs. D. D. Spencer, in 1902.

PLATE XLIII   *Courtesy of Mrs. Flo E. Flintjer*

CROSS-PATCH

An original design by Carrie A. Hall, developed from a crossword puzzle and made of blue print, plain blue, and white. A
very unusual quilt.

PLATE XLIV   *Collection of Thayer Museum*

This quilt belonged to the family of Alexander Hamilton. It is
made of dull brown and cream squares of glazed chintz with a
delicate design. The edge is finished with a hand-made fringe.

PLATE XLV   *Collection of Thayer Museum*

TREE OF LIFE

Homespun muslin, appliqued with an elaborate design cut from glazed chintz. A wide band of chintz forms the border. The quilt is very old and is from the collection of Colonel Dyer, a Kansas City pioneer.

THE PATCHWORK QUILT

There was a wind in the night—a little hurried sigh:
And in the morning someone moved among the trees,
Tall, with hair that blew from clouds to earth.
And on her arm there hung a basket,
Deep, and wide, and ancient,
Waiting to be filled.

There came a thought of mists and night-frosts;
Of chilly waters creeping through grass unheralded;
Of footprints leading home.
The leaves tossed sleepily and fell,
And as they fell she gathered them into her basket,
And in a shaft of amber-tinted light
She set herself to make a coverlet, patch by patch—
Green leaves, golden leaves,
Tawny, brown, auburn, and scarlet—
To spread across the countryside and keep it warm.
Never was seen so fine a patchwork quilt
As Autumn stitched that day.

D. A. LOVELL.

PLATE XLVI   *Collection of Thayer Museum*

THE KITE'S TAIL

The running line of squares are alternately dark red and blue.
The vine in the border is green with red flowers. This is a nine-
teenth century reproduction of a quilt in the "dower-chest" of
Jane Roan of Lancaster, Pa., 1778.

PLATE XLVII   *Collection of Thayer Museum*

LOG CABIN
An antique quilt. The calico and the design indicate its age.

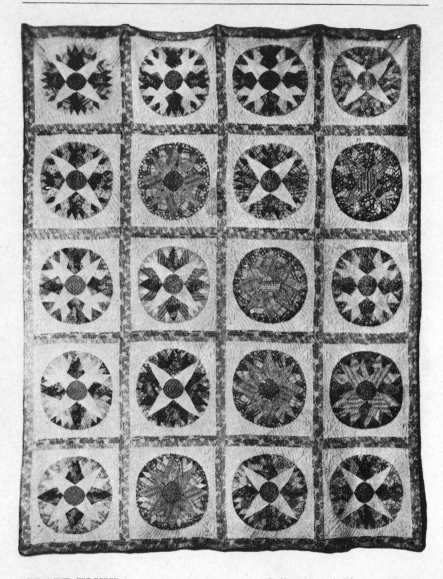

CHIPS AND WHETSTONES
Made by Susannah Richards Mosely, Pembroke, Kentucky, in 1850.

PLATE XLIX   *Collection of Thayer Museum*

ROSE OF SHARON
Made by Rena Coon Thomas, Sharon, Illinois, in 1860.   Quite
unlike the usual "Rose of Sharon" design.

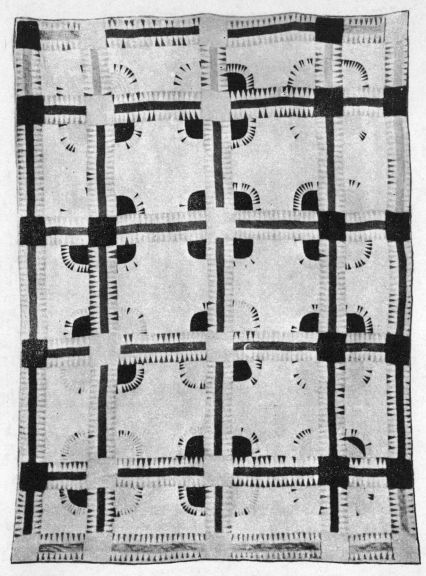

PLATE L   *Collection of Thayer Museum*

ROCKY MOUNTAIN ROAD
Made by Mrs. Wm. H. Dorey in Kentucky. The quilt shows
that it has been in constant use as it is worn and faded. The
original colors were red and white. It was given the Thayer
Museum by Mrs. A. J. Anderson, who is a great-niece of the
maker.

IN A MUSEUM

Rare old quilt, of faded hue—
Once a bride's most precious treasure
Hidden in her dower-chest.
Loving hands that fashioned you
Stitch by stitch, in careful measure
Long ago, are now at rest.

Your patches tell a wondrous story
Of treasured scraps and handicraft;
Of love and home, and dreams come true.
For honored guests your pattern'd glory,
Enfolding them, caressing, soft—
And baby hands have lightly touched you.

Now you're worth your weight in gold;
To lie in state your only duty,
In pleasant ways your lot is cast
And to the world your tale is told.
To those who love your patterned beauty
You re-create the fragrant past.

                    CARRIE A. HALL.

PLATE LI   *Collection of Thayer Museum*

FLOWER BASKETS
Made by a great-aunt of Mrs. A. J. Anderson of Lawrence,
Kansas. A very old family pattern.

PLATE LII   *Courtesy of Miss Lillian Constant*

WREATH OF FLOWERS

Made in 1858 by Harriett Grabendike who, at the age of sixteen, gathered flowers and leaves from the garden, placed them in a large wreath, and copied the design for her quilt. The large roses in the corners and center of the quilt are seven layers of material, including the leaves, and are appliqued on with button-hole stitch. The colors are pink, red, light and dark green, and orange, and remain almost perfect in tint. The quilting required two weeks' time and six two-hundred yard spools of cotton thread. It is very beautiful and complicated, being roses, feathers, diamonds, with curved and straight lines for fillers. This quilt is a fine contribution to early American art and is owned by a daughter of Mrs. Harriett (Grabendike) Constant.

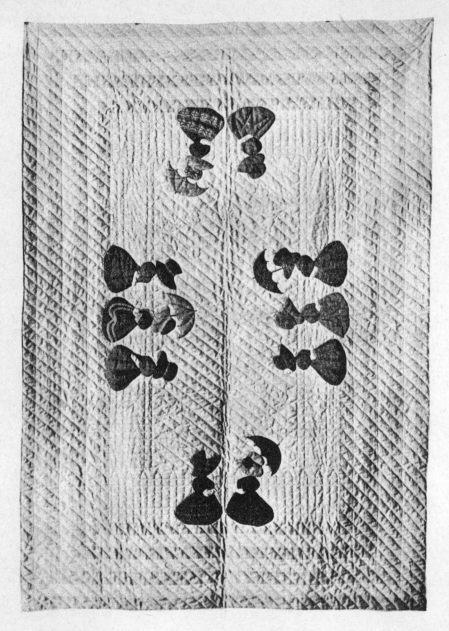

CHILD'S QUILT
Adapted from a Webster pattern by Carrie A. Hall, in 1925.

CHILD'S QUILT
Embroidered animal design.

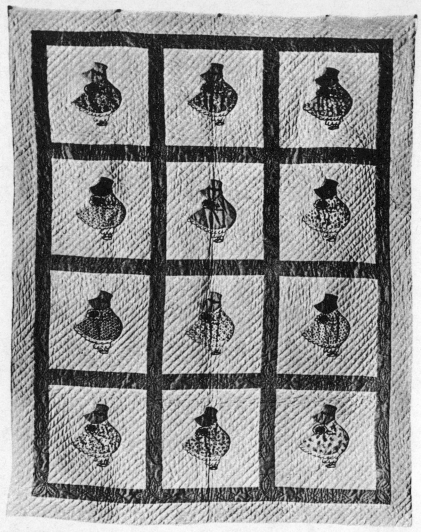

PLATE LV   *Courtesy of Mrs. H. S. Stevenson*

SUN-BONNET BABY QUILT
These cunning little dresses are made of scraps of the dainty
frocks of a small daughter.

PLATE LVI   *Courtesy of Mrs. H. S. Stevenson*

HONEY BEE
A beautiful specimen of this lovely old colonial pattern.

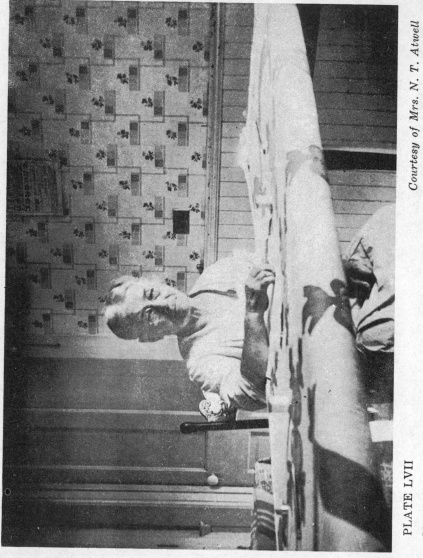

PLATE LVII

Mrs. Atwell at work. Several quilts reproduced in this book are the work of her skillful fingers. See the orchid satin quilt in Plate CXIII.

Courtesy of Mrs. N. T. Atwell

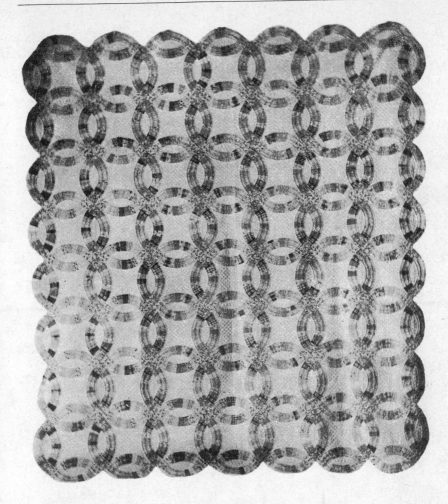

DOUBLE WEDDING RING
A very fine example of this popular old pattern.

PLATE LIX   *Courtesy of Miss Dickey*

FEATHER STAR
Note the interesting Saw Tooth border.

PLATE LX   *Courtesy of Mrs. Clara Cloud*

OAK LEAF AND CURRANT
A very old quilt with an interesting border, developed in
green and red.

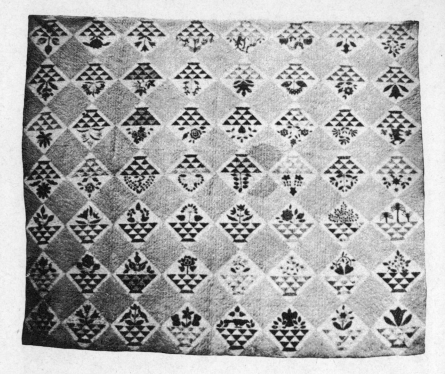

PLATE LXI   *Courtesy of Mrs. Howard Wittleib*

BASKET QUILT
An unusual example of this very old favorite pattern. Note
that each basket has a different variety of flowers. No quilt
collection of our grandmother's day was complete without a
basket quilt.

PLATE LXII   *Courtesy of Mrs. Howard Wittleib*

LOG CABIN
A very old woolen quilt of the type known as "Barn Raising."

PLATE LXIII   *Courtesy of Mrs. Caldwell*

EGYPTIAN LOTUS FLOWER
A most unusual design developed in red, green, and yellow.

TULIP QUILT
Made by the owner's mother, Mrs. Sarah Elma Seacrist-Charles, Marion, Indiana, in 1859. A very beautiful quilt with an interesting and unusual border.

PLATE LXV   *Courtesy of Miss Lulu Charles*

WREATH OF GARDEN FLOWERS

Made by the owner's mother, Mrs. Sarah Elma Seacrist-Charles,
Marion, Indiana, in 1859. This is an unusually dainty design of
excellent workmanship. The border design is very fine.

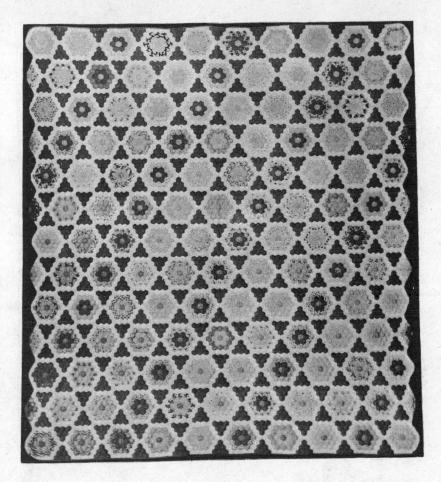

GRANDMOTHER'S FLOWER GARDEN

A modern quilt made by the owner in 1930. Over eight thousand hexagons make this beautiful quilt.

PLATE LXVII   *Courtesy of Mrs. Louise Atkinson*

CALIFORNIA PLUME

This picture shows Mrs. Atkinson and her cherished "California Plume" quilt, made by Mrs. Charity Atkinson, her mother-in-law, and given to her as a wedding present in 1870. Taken at her home where she has lived for the past sixty-two years on an original grant of land near Kickapoo, Kansas. The evening before this picture was taken, a terrific hailstorm broke all the windows and otherwise damaged the house. Note the battered appearance of the roof. Mrs. Atkinson is over eighty years old and is listed by the Kansas State Historical Society as the oldest living pioneer woman in Kansas, having been brought to Kansas by her parents, David and Mary Schwartz, in 1852 when she was only three months old.

GRANDMOTHER'S QUILT

"Some day,
We will have a square for you."
She would say; and to me, standing by her knee
In that old-fashioned sitting room
With its forgotten horsehair,
Flowered carpeting,
And firelit hearth
Of childhood memory,
She would explain
That homemade tapestry:

"That pretty printed one
Was once your mother's dress;
The pink, Aunt Julia's,
And the blue, a shirt of Uncle Will's;
While all the corners were begun
With Kansas scraps Aunt Hannah sent
From where the Indians live,
Beneath the prairie sun;
And that old piece of fancy cloth
Was Uncle Albert's vest,
And all those fill-ins at the seams
Were ties of Grandpa's,
Long, long years ago——"

But mine—I thought with childlike dreams—
Should be a very large square,
And of pink brocade;
When I had become great and made
The whole wide world
To tremble at my name!
When I would have fame,
And be as high as the topmost steeple
Of the village spires,
When from all lands would come the people
Just to hear me sing.
Then would Grandmother bring
From out its lavender that quilt of yore,
And pointing to that pink brocade
Square of gorgeousness,
Say, with prideful happiness,
"This . . . my famous grandchild wore!"

But now—
If only she may find
Upon my quilt of life,
A little, humble patch of white—
Of righteousness.

SARAH WILSON MIDDLETON.

PLATE LXVIII   *Courtesy of Mrs. G. W. Vaughn*

THE LABYRINTH
An original design by Carrie A. Hall and developed in dark and
light green, green print, and white. A most beautiful and unusual quilt.

Love in these labyrinths his slaves detains.
                              ALEXANDER POPE.

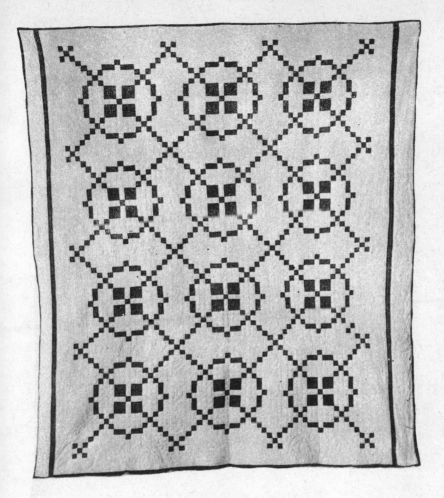

PLATE LXIX   *Courtesy of Millie Shaw Hamlin*

BURGOYNE SURROUNDED
Made by the owner's grandmother, Marie Kinmore, Tomah, Wisconsin, in 1857. Colors: red and white.

PLATE LXX   *Collection of Mrs. A. L. Withers*

DELECTABLE MOUNTAINS
A variation of the original Delectable Mountains pattern made
by Mrs. C. B. Withers in 1900. Copied from an old quilt made
in Virginia and in the family for over one hundred years.

PLATE LXXI   *Collection of Mrs. A. L. Withers*

SILK CRAZY QUILT

A fine example of this type of quilt that was so popular in the
latter part of the nineteenth century. Note the date, the motto,
and the many varieties of beautiful and elaborate embroidery.
A wide border of red plush is elaborately embroidered with
chenille flowers.

PLATE LXXII   *Courtesy of Mrs. Bert Wilson*

SLASHED FEATHER STAR
Developed in mustard green print and white. Note the "Wild
Goose Chase" effect in the border.

PLATE LXXIII   *Courtesy of Mrs. Bert Wilson*

ROSE APPLIQUE
An unusual Rose design with a spray border growing out of
urns. Made of scraps of all kinds of print. Very old.

PLATE LXXIV   *Courtesy of "A Friend."*

PRESIDENT'S WREATH
Very old. Colors: red and green.

PLATE LXXV   *Courtesy of Mrs. Roger Moon*

ORIGINAL WHIG ROSE
An interesting border design and elaborate quilting.

PLATE LXXVI   *Collection of Mrs. Charlotte Jane Whitehill*

Reproduction of "Old English Rose" combined with "Kentucky Rose." A modern quilt with border design by the owner.

PLATE LXXVII   *Collection of Mrs. Charlotte Jane Whitehill*

COLONIAL ROSE QUILT
A modern reproduction of an early Colonial design.

PLATE LXXVIII   *Collection of Mrs. Charlotte Jane Whitehill*

TULIP QUILT
Made by the owner's mother in 1855.

PLATE LXXIX   *Collection of Mrs. Charlotte Jane Whitehill*

PEONY

Made by the owner's mother in 1857. The flowers are pieced
of diamonds.

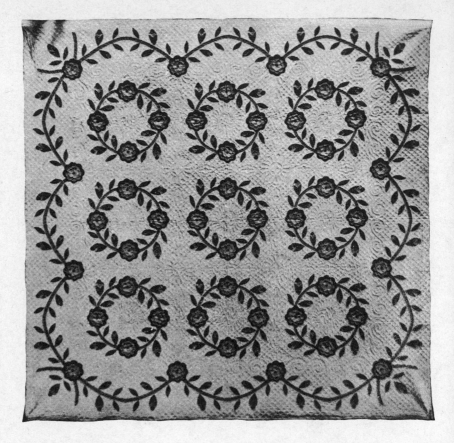

PLATE LXXX   *Collection of Mrs. S. H. Rich*

THE KENTUCKY ROSE
A very old quilt with interesting border and quilting designs.

BEAUTY

She follows many a devious path,
Interprets many a mood;
Triumphant walks the city's street,
Companions solitude:

Not only in gilt palaces
We trace her garment's hem;
Earth's lowliest ones may call to her
And she will come to them,

In cloud, or wave, or song of bird,
In flower, prairie, tree;
In any spot, through any task
Done with sincerity,—

A furrow straight across a field,
A rose-tree by the door;
A blossomy quilt upon a bed,
Quaint rugs upon a floor!

JEAN CROSSE HANSEN

INDIAN PAINT BRUSH
Original old quilt. Colors: orange and green. Made in 1852.

PLATE LXXXII   *Collection of Mrs. S. H. Rich*

A modern reproduction of the Indian Paint Brush shown in Plate LXXXI with original border design by Mrs. Rich. Quilting designs specially fitted to the open spaces.

PLATE LXXXIII   *Collection of Mrs. S. H. Rich*

DEMOCRAT ROSE
An original border design by Mrs. Rich and interesting background quilting.

PLATE LXXXIV

MY MOTHER'S STAR

Reproduced from a quilt made in Kansas in 1868 by Mrs.
Hannah Rich. Red, green and yellow.

PLATE LXXXV   *Collection of Mrs. S. H. Rich*

YOUNG MAN'S FANCY or GOOSE-IN-THE-POND
A reproduction of a quilt pieced by Mr. Rich's mother. It re-
called such happy childhood memories that Mr. Rich begged the
privilege of quilting it himself.

PLATE LXXXVI

Courtesy of Mrs. Jennie Markwell

SUNSHINE AND SHADOW
A modern quilt of very unusual pattern containing thirty-six
hundred pieces.

PLATE LXXXVII   *Courtesy of Mrs. H. M. Cushman*

FEATHER ROSE
Made by Hannah Ehlers about 1880. A very beautiful combination of rose and feather patterns in red and green.

PLATE LXXXVIII   *Courtesy of Mrs. H. M. Cushman*

PINEAPPLE

Made about 1870 by Hannah Ehlers (now Mrs. Cushman). She saw a quilt of this design at a fair at a little village called Camp Point, near Quincy, Illinois. A friend procured the pattern for her, having to pay $1.25 for it. It is made entirely of wool and not quilted. Each piece in the block having a different shape, it required painstaking care in cutting and piecing to make so perfect a quilt. The light color is challis and of a color known in those days as "buff."

PLATE LXXXIX   *Courtesy of Miss Hazel Watkins*

BROKEN STAR

Made by the owner's mother, Mrs. Emma Watkins, age seventy-
two years. Colors are orange, turkey red, dark green, and old-
fashioned pink. A very beautiful specimen of this lovely
pattern, and of excellent workmanship.

PLATE XC   *Courtesy of Mrs. Carlotta Wettack*

WHEEL OF FORTUNE
Made of figured blue and black calico, and a turkey red calico
with yellow flowers, which have worn out showing the cotton
filling. An interesting Saw Tooth border. Date not known, but
general appearance and design of calico would place it c. 1840.

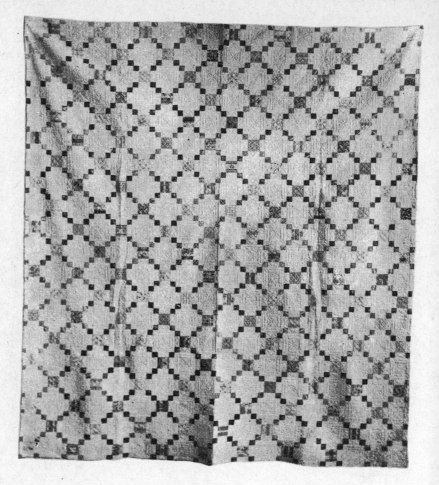

PLATE XCI   *Courtesy of Mrs. William Johnston*

OLD NINE-PATCH QUILT

Made by Mrs. Johnston's aunt, Mrs. Lucy Bradbury, Niles, Michigan. Mrs. Bradbury began the quilt in 1831, but the family home was so small there was no extra room to put the quilt up for quilting so it was not finished until 1858. Counting ten hours a day's work, it took thirty-six days and six spools of thread for the quilting, which is most interesting as to design and of finest workmanship. The quilt has been Mrs. Johnston's prized possession for more than thirty years.

PLATE XCII   *Courtesy of Mrs. William Johnston*

SILK CRAZY QUILT

This quilt was made several years ago from various badges
Mrs. Johnston, wife of Chief Justice Johnston of the Supreme
Court of Kansas, has received from conventions where she
acted as delegate from the numerous organizations to which she
belongs. Also badges to receptions for notables, etc. You will
see one badge with a sunflower, in the center of which is a picture of ex-Vice President Curtis. Another one marked LL.D.
Oxford, 1921, her college and the honorary degree conferred
upon her.

PLATE XCIII   *Courtesy of Ida M. Bartleson*

CALIFORNIA ROSE
Made by Mrs. Eliza S. Tarr in 1854, now owned by J. W.
Bartleson of Beloit, Kansas.

PLATE XCIV   *Courtesy of Ida M. Bartleson*

TEXAS STAR

Made by Mary Anderson Bartleson in 1867. This quilt has
survived the westward progress of the family and after being
"at home" in fourteen different homes en route, is now the
treasured possession of J. W. Bartleson, of Beloit, Kansas.
(See Part I, Plate XXXV, No. 8, called Cottage Tulips.)

PINEAPPLE
Made by Mrs. Eliza Srician in Mitchell County, Kansas in 1880.
Colors: blue and white. Now owned by Carrie McClintic.
Very attractive quilting.

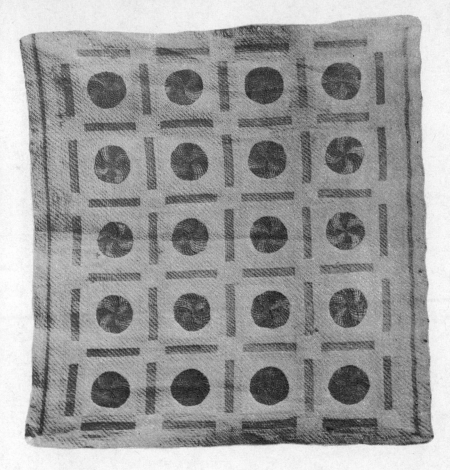

PLATE XCVI   *Courtesy of Carrie McClintic*

SPINNING BALL

Made of green and red calicos in Kentucky about 1850 by Mrs.
Mobala Logan. It is made and quilted with hand-spun linen
thread made in the Logan home. The colors are clear and
unfaded.

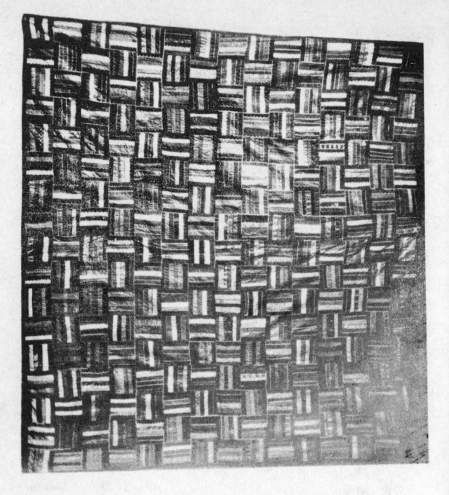

PLATE XCVII   *Courtesy of Mrs. Loretta Selover*

ROMAN SQUARE
A very beautiful silk quilt reproduced from an old pattern.
Made by the owner. (See Part I, Plate II, No. 10.)

PLATE XCVIII   *Courtesy of Mrs. S. W. Durant*

BLUE WREATH QUILT

A very simple yet unusual design made by Alice Tandy in
Illinois in 1865. A white flower with a yellow center is set upon
a larger patch of deep, dark blue the color of her soldier lover's
uniform.

PLATE XCIX   *Collection of Rose G. Kretsinger*

DOUBLE IRISH CHAIN
Made by Mrs. Anna G. Good, mother of Mrs. Rose G. Kretsinger. The colors: lavender and pink in the chain are softly
blended and the thistles are red with green leaves.

PLATE C   *Collection of Mrs. Rose G. Kretsinger*

SNOW CRYSTALS
This is an interesting example of an old-time pattern that is
sometimes called "Yankee Pride" and has a "Wild-Goose-Chase"
border.

PLATE CI   *Collection of Mrs. Rose G. Kretsinger*

WREATH OF ROSES
Reproduction of an old pattern with an original border design
and specially adapted quilting designs.

PLATE CII   *Collection of Mrs. Rose G. Kretsinger*

OHIO ROSE
Reproduced in red and white check gingham, also red, green,
and black. (See Part I, Plate XXXII, No. 10.)

PLATE CIII   *Collection of Mrs. Rose G. Kretsinger*

ANTIQUE ROSE

The original quilt, from the fragments of which this was reproduced, was almost completely destroyed in the Chicago fire of
1871. Colors, green, three shades of red, and black.

PLATE CIV   *Collection of Mrs. Rose G. Kretsinger*

ORIENTAL POPPY

Reproduced from a fragment in the same "hope chest" as Plate CIII. Colors are red, pink, and green. Note the Saw Tooth outline around the patches and the elaborate border. The background quilting serves to enhance the beauty of the design.

PLATE CV   *Collection of Mrs. Rose G. Kretsinger*

PRIDE OF IOWA
A nineteenth century pattern reproduced in original details and
coloring, to which has been added an interesting border design
with specially designed quilting motifs.

PLATE CVII   *Collection of Mrs. Rose G. Kretsinger*

INDIANA WREATH
An adaptation of the quilt shown by Marie D. Webster as
frontispiece in her book, with a specially designed quilting
pattern. The naturalistic coloring is most beautifully blended.

PLATE CVIII   *Collection of Mrs. Rose G. Kretsinger*

CALENDULA

A very fine specimen of stuffed quilting. The interlaced ring
patches and the border are original designs and the motifs for
quilting were especially designed. Colors are canary yellow,
orange, and mustard green. This quilt has taken first prize
at the Kansas State Fair.

PLATE CIX   *Collection of Mrs. Rose G. Kretsinger*

ROSE TREE

This is a modern version of a very old pattern with original
center and border swag. The quilting designs were made specially for this quilt. (See Plate XIV.)

PLATE CX   *Collection of Mrs. Rose G. Kretsinger*

ORCHID WREATH

This quilt, in design, color scheme, and quilting is entirely original and is Mrs. Kretsinger's most beautiful creation. It is a veritable "picture of patches." The colors used are several shades of purple, three shades of green, yellow, pink, cerise, and black. The artistic color combination and the exquisite needlework is too fine to show in the photograph. It must be seen to be appreciated. Mrs. Kretsinger, an artist in many other lines as well as with the needle, has made all of the quilts in her collection.

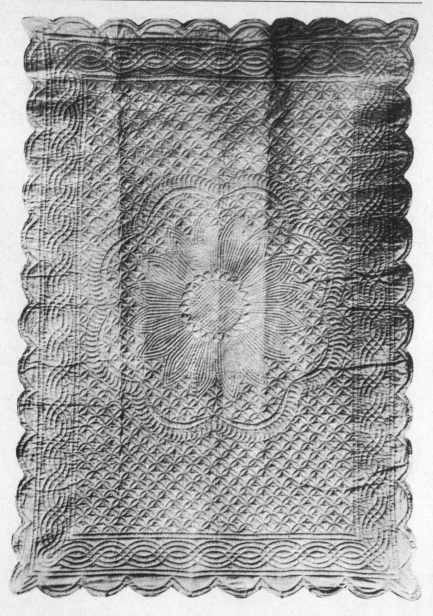

PLATE CXI   *Collection of Mrs. W. A. Jeffers*

Rose sateen is the foundation for this elaborate quilted design.
The Kansas Sunflower forms the center motif.

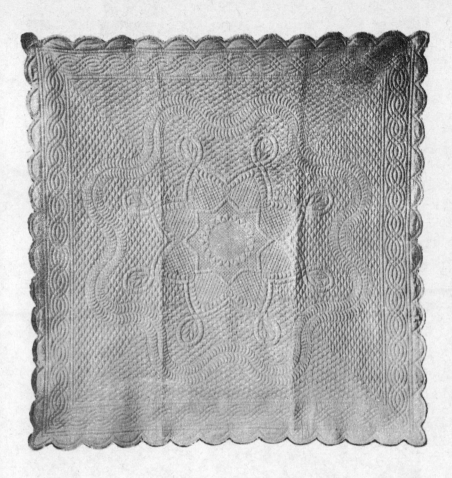

PLATE CXII   *Collection of Mrs. W. A. Jeffers*

A very elaborate white sateen quilt with a beautiful star motif
quilted in the center.

PLATE CXIII   *Courtesy of Mrs. Clarence Ryan*

Orchid satin quilt with wool filling, designed and quilted by
Mrs. N. T. Atwell.

PLATE CXIV   *Courtesy of Mrs. Ferris Hill*

A treasured example of an antique stuffed quilt showing the
center motif. The stuffed border outlines the entire quilt.

PLATE CXV   *Courtesy of the granddaughter of Mrs. S. W. Durant*

A very fine example of an all-white stuffed quilt made in Illinois in 1865 by Mrs. Alice Tandy. Quilting was the "play-time" of this pioneer woman. After she had put the children (nine of them) to bed, she would take her recreation in making beautiful quilts.

PLATE CXVI   *Collection of Thayer Museum*

A beautiful example of the quilter's art on green-homespun
linen. Note the great variety of designs.

PLATE CXVII   *Collection of Thayer Museum*

This is a fine example of stuffed quilting. Both top and lining
are of homespun linen. Every design is stuffed and the surface
is so well covered that no background quilting is necessary. The
initials B.H.B. are quilted on the left-hand side near the top.

PLATE CXVIII   *Collection of Thayer Museum*

This is a perfect example of stuffed quilting, with a finely
quilted background.   Made by Elizabeth Holmes Adams of
Petersboro, New Hampshire, in 1820.

PLATE CXIX

This quilt is an adaptation of a design by Mary Evangeline
Walker in honor of the George Washington bi-centennial. The
silhouette of Washington with bunches of cherries in red and
green, and the dates "1732" and "1932" in blue, form a framed
medallion in the center of the quilt surrounded by a row of
hatchets. The cherry trees are in red and green and the band
of mosaics are in blue and white, representing the pavements
of Washington, D. C.

Part 3

The Art of Quilting and Quilting Designs

To my mother
ANNA GLEISSNER GOOD

INTRODUCTION

A number of interesting articles have been written recently concerning quilting, both old and new, and exhaustive illustrations offered to people interested in reviving this artistic ancient craft; to these special writers I acknowledge my great indebtedness for the encouragement I have received and also for the helpful information regarding the early work of both European and Colonial quilters.

ROSE G. KRETSINGER.

1

THE ART OF QUILTING

EVERYONE loves the quilt, and everyone knows what quilting is, since for centuries it has been an art traditionally practiced by the women of many lands. It still holds one of the most popular, prominent, and important positions in all needlecraft, because of its lasting beauty and fine decorative features. If studied as an applied art, and properly understood, it is not only capable of a high development, but is in itself a vast field for the display of individual taste and self-expression. It fills even a more useful, practical, and intimate place in our domestic life than embroidery and becomes more fascinating inasmuch as it gives women, by their own handiwork, a chance for artistic and tasteful adornment of their homes. The practicability and usefulness of quilted things and the joy and pride derived from creating things for everyday use, should be an incentive to every domestic housewife to make and own at least one good quilt.

Quilting is one of the oldest forms of needlework, and became popular in Europe as early as the Eleventh Century. It was later introduced into the new world by the Dutch and English colonists, whose primary object it was to found homes. One can readily see how quilting flourished amid such favorable circumstances.

In the development of quilting, women have ever played an important part. Within their needlework we find the story of their very existence, and that of the country wherein they live. By the artistic character of their productions we may judge of the mental development of the people and of their domestic conditions. More than any other American antique, does the quilt or quilted garment hold a particular appeal by reason of its quaint romance intermingled with homespun days. We associate it with the infant tucked in the crib, the little girl's first needlework, the artistic creation for the marriage chest, the bride's special touch of decoration for the guest-room bed, and at last it becomes the heirloom of the family to be cherished until worn to threads.

Throughout the years, numbers of these quilted treasures have lain packed within ancestral chests and almost forgotten, until someone with artistic predilection happens to discover and appreciate them for their irresistibly quaint beauty, and again they have been brought out to be displayed and admired, each object telling its story of the long ago.

There were no schools of design open to our pioneer mothers, and for the most part, her patterns were of quite simple geometric shapes, many of them having been used for generations. Occasionally a very ambitious quilter turned to the garden for inspiration, creating some beautiful and unusual floral design of admirable and lasting charm. Some have conceived motifs from the birds, since birds have offered limitless numbers of ideas to designers ever since ancient times and artists will ever continue to be inspired by them. Even the single feather of the bird has proved a charming well for the flow of design. Feathers such as that of the peacock or ostrich having unusual form or markings lends tone and line rhythm to the variations of the pattern.

In many cases it is difficult to know from what bird or plant a designer has derived his idea, but it is the privilege of the artist to think first of satisfactory grouping and mass arrangement in order to enhance the beauty of line in the design. In so doing the realistic may entirely be lost.

In reviewing some of the old specimens of quilting displayed in our museums and private collections, we stand amazed at the manifestations of harmonious form and order, when in those strenuous times there were so few advantages offered our foremothers. Through the necessity of man, which concerns the maintenance of life itself, the quilt became one of the most utilitarian commodities of household use and great numbers of them were made.

Very soon women learned to fill in their spare moments with needlework, and quilting at once became both a social and pastime accomplishment, growing more artistic through increasing competition in the art. No doubt the early quilting, like the patchwork itself, was stitched upon simple bed coverings, made for pure utility; but the love of beautiful things and self-expression seemed entirely regardless of all difficulty, and since the pioneer woman could not live in luxury, she made a desperate effort, at least, not to live in ugliness. As a result, quilting developed, not only in a utilitarian, but also in an artistic way. With their skillful fingers women created from homespun fabric treasures of elaborate quilting, which have come down to us as master needlework. In the early days, the one aim and ambition of the Colonial woman seemed towards increasing the efficiency and happiness of life. Her stitches were lasting and executed with a loving hand, with disregard for length of time involved in the accomplishment. Today, although there seems to be a marked interest and revival of quilting, yet there is also a feeling of commercialization which tends towards lowering its sincerity and individuality as needle art. Women are depending more upon the printed pattern sheet to save time and labor. These, having been used time and again, often become very tiresome.

Even so, the times seem to have changed since art training and appreciation was confined to the few talented people. It is today recognized as an element of necessity in every modern home and enables us to realize more perfectly the joy of living. It is the desire of everyone to possess and to create beautiful things. It is born in every child, just as his desire for food, so that unconsciously he reaches out for the thing which pleases through the eye and which satisfies his natural craving for beauty. This divine instinct should be encouraged and properly directed, for it depicts part of man's emotional nature, and enters into the business of life wherein we are all most interested. It is the expression of personal individuality and character. It uplifts our thought beyond the commonplace and sordid things in life, without disregard for our practical and domestic needs. Beautiful things appeal to the emotions and create a sort of mental state of quiet and spiritual goodness. Why, then, should we live without this understanding, when it is so essential to humanity and reveals to such a marked degree the extent of culture and refinement of the home?

All of us, at times, have been carried away by the sight of some beautiful art object, and to arouse this feeling by what one is able to create, proves the practicability of acquiring some training in selection and arrangement, the fundamentals of applied design.

It has been said by different disinterested people: "Why spend so much time and labor making new quilts and worrying about designs when you already have a number which are never used?" Perhaps it is for the same reason which prompts the planting of flowers in the alley, back of the garden fence, or the landscaping of our gardens in places seen only by the few; because of our love for beauty and regard for order in everyday living. It is in us and must come forth and become a material artistic expression. We may not at first attain the desired results, but it is only human and natural to yield to the impulse which gives attention to the appearances of things all about us.

In quilting as in all other lines, the highest type of artistry has come only through patience, practice, and study with a careful observation of the accumulated experiences of quilters of both past and modern days. Every woman can sew, but quilting is something beyond mere stitching. It is a means of expressing line rhythm and artistic forms upon materials. We might even liken the quilt to musical composition. It has its high and low color tones, and its swelling and diminishing line rhythm; all carrying the eye through a design composition. The quilter, if artist, should be absolute master and control the needle, for stitches, so to speak, are the language of the art and of almost first importance. Fineness and intricacy of stitching are its character features.

One often finds a most indifferent and commonplace specimen of patch or applique enriched to the extent of a masterpiece by the exquisiteness and artistry of the quilter. On the other hand, a most elegant quilt top may be ruined by ignorance or careless indifference in quilting. The branches of applied arts are so related and so dependent upon each other that the success we have with one is nearly always in proportion to the knowledge we have of the other. This is especially noticeable in quilt-making, for the several types of work, quilting, designing, and color, each giving sanction for such variation in style and treatment, may, if not properly combined with regard for appropriateness, prove successful as a unit. Perhaps this is the reason few women have had the inclination, courage, or skill to make a really good quilt, from start to finish—designing, piecing, and quilting. It is possible for any artistic needlewoman to do so. If she has ability in one line of applied art, she is not without talent in others, and it would seem that after months in the work of producing a design of patch or lovely applique, it would be a temptation to complete the entire piece of work, by also doing the quilting. Instead, the quilt top is made by one person, then passed on to some other worker to be quilted. Perhaps not every woman has a quilting frame, or room enough to set one up for such a long time. Unlike the piece-work, the quilting must be confined to one place until finished; while the quilt top may be carried anywhere in the process of making. Then, I have had quilters tell of their sore fingers and other discomforts of the work, which would certainly be anything but an encouragement to the average modern woman.

In the last few years there has been a sort of universal enthusiasm for quilting, which has prompted the making of many different things in both modernistic and old colonial modes. These, especially the counterpanes, have attracted widespread favorable attention of quilters and of those who appreciate quilts as interesting art objects. In a great many cases, however, these articles for household use are made from unsubstantial materials, simply to produce an effect of quality and to answer a sort of decorative purpose, more than that of lasting needlework. For example, I make mention of the modern quilted boudoir accessories, cushions, etc., which are so familiar to all of us, and may be purchased as stamped and ready to work products in all department stores. They are in colored rayon, made to affect a satin elegance, when in reality they are quite unenduring, materially, artistically, and in workmanship. It requires little or no skill to quilt, with embroidery thread, the long stitches indicated to outline the simple floral or scroll pattern. Some of these designs have backgrounds quilted after the old diamond pattern so well known and in constant use. Others have plain quilted backgrounds with the design brought into high relief by inserting a large cord, as the work progresses. Although this modern type of quilting has no serious merit, it still finds its way into every home in village, town, and city, because

PLATE B

A small portion of a Quilted Coverlet, probably of Sicilian work. Date about 1400. This specimen may be seen at the Victoria Albert Museum in London.

of the little difficulty encountered in the making. What a pity, for it would be really more worth while to spend years in the making of one good piece of quilting than the time it takes to quilt all the other inartistic ones. We are always well repaid in making something lovely, for "A thing of beauty is a joy forever."

In the days before the advent of the sewing machine into American domestic life, it was a necessity for every young woman to know how to do really fine and beautiful hand stitching. This accomplishment constituted an essential part of her education, just as did literature, music, and etiquette. Very early she was taught her first stitches on the sampler of the nine-patch square; and later, as her advancing knowledge would permit, the more complicated types of stitching, such as the quilting of bonnets, petticoats, gowns, and other things for personal use. When not busily engaged in the making of the necessary supply of clothing, it was her one object and ambition to prepare a well-filled marriage chest for her future use. This necessitated years in the making of hand-stitched needlework. Each piece represented untiring skill and artistic ability. It is from rare collections of this kind that the fortunate antiquarian comes across some of the best quilted pieces which later find place in our museums. The old white stuffed counterpane, the quilted petticoat or bonnet, these ancestral pieces are scarce, but connoisseurs are diligently hunting for them and once in a great while an exceptionally elusive piece is discovered in perchance an antique shop, or in some neighbor friend's old trunk; but no matter how worn or frayed, if it happens by chance to be the old stuffed type of quilting, it is a rare prize. This unusual style is raised into bas-relief by the stuffing of cotton into the floral or scroll ornamentation. To achieve this each segment of the design must be perforated with a stilletto from the wrong side, making a small hole, through which cotton is inserted until the space within is filled. The threads, having been merely separated, are then pushed carefully together again without breaking the fabric. At times, the background of such work is solidly quilted, leaving almost no spacing between the lines of stitching. Quilting of this kind is almost always found on antique quilts, for seldom have our modern women time or nervous energy to stay by the quilting frame long enough to complete a piece of work of this kind even though highly paid for executing the work.

One of the rare specimens of stuffed quilting may be seen at the Victoria Albert Museum in London. It is of foreign needlecraft, although it resembles numerous of the early American ones in technique. It was made in Sicily about 1400. The quilting is designed to depict scenes from the life of Tristam, who often engaged in battle against King Sanguis. Bits of floral scroll and lettering run through the design. In this fine old piece of work, the material is of buff-colored linen and the raised motifs are obtained by stuffing with wool. Close irregular quilting fills in the background almost solidly, giving a flat tooled effect. To outline the figures, the quilter has employed the use of brown thread to accentuate the pattern.

As in this quilted coverlet, colored thread has been used in many other cases in early American work. Some quilters have combined both embroidery and quilting. At times verses or mottoes have been quilted into the design in color.

Although quilting has been a needlecraft in general use nearly everywhere for centuries, and its constructive principles have been much the same, yet the technique of design and materials used seem quite individual to the people of each land. This is noticeable in English Elizabethan quilting, which was done on silk, satin, fine linens, and cloth of gold, showing striking contrast to the modest simplicity of materials used in our early Colonial days, which depict the unadorned background of the serious, hard-working mothers.

In France, quilting was not as generally used as in England, although much was being done. It was not of an elaborate style of design, and confined chiefly to the peasant class living in the southern section of the country, in the neighborhood of Arles, Avignon, and Nimes. Here the quilted skirt or jupon was featured in the costume worn by the women, when each locality had its own individual type of dress. These petticoats were styled in voluminous, rippling fullness, at times four yards around, and gathered at the waist. The material was of the fine French cotton chintz, with printed patterns of trailing vines and flowers on a white-, blue-, or saffron-colored background. Heavily padded with wadding, they were quilted solidly with close diamond or hanging diamond patterns (Quilting Plate I), and with banding of straight line quilting at the bottom to form a border. Occasionally flower bandings were used in border quiltings, but not often. The jupon dated back two hundred years or more and continued to be popular until 1860, at which time the fashions changed and the custom of provincial costume went out. The jupons were then laid carefully away in chest or cupboard until some other use could be made of the great lengths of lovely quilted material, which represented such worlds of needlework. Some thrifty housewives at once converted them into coverlets by sewing two lengths together, with the border bandings on two sides; others cherished them only as beautiful old garments, and at length they became family relics, until of recent years, when here and there a lovely quilted jupon has been discovered and purchased by tourist or decorator. Soon all collectors were eagerly seeking them for their artistic possibilities and they found rapid sale in both French and American exclusive shops.

It was through the discovery of the French quilted jupon that quilted coverings for old furniture came into vogue, and the little quilted boudoir pillows, made from the scraps of material left after covering the chair or couch. These gay old petticoats were not only used to upholster furniture, but because of their lovely, picturesque, and colorful patterns, were put to many other uses; boudoir jackets, portieres, and drapes of different kinds. Their age-mellowed texture could so easily be combined with the antique style of furniture universally used at that time.

Quilted petticoats were also in general use here in America and popular with the Dutch women of the colonies. They were not only works of art in finely stitched quilting, but served the purpose of necessary warmth, in the cold, rigorous New England winters, when homes were not well heated. It was not unusual for the women to possess numbers of them. Some were made from expensive and beautiful fabrics but few remain to tell the tale, for in the process of constant wear and during the needy times of long, hard struggle for independence in our land, they gradually disappeared. It is rare when by chance we find one of these treasured antiques at the present time. But it seems strange how those who love and appreciate beautiful things will find them when they are least expecting to.

PLATE C

A quilted petticoat of the style in general use in America in Colonial times. Courtesy of Thayer Museum.

And now at this busy time in our history we are growing tired of machine-made things, and women are turning more and more toward the old Colonial arts. Special effort is being made to revive the antique patterns and technique of hand-weaving and quaint needlecrafts, of which quilting is perhaps one of the most outstanding and highly appreciated of them all. Even the men stop to reminisce when they see a quilt displayed. One man whom I happen to know has been interested enough in his wife's quilt-making to assist in the quilting of a pattern which belonged to his mother, the work being rendered the more interesting by the use of her original quilting frame which had lain away in the attic of their ancestral home these many years.

It has been my good fortune during the past few years to discover a few very interesting old quilting designs, most of which I have used in my quilt-making. These, with a few original ones, I wish to place before you in a set of fifteen plates. My purpose is not competitive in any way, but to show what has been accomplished in quilting design and to add from my own practical experience such knowledge as may help the interested quilter, and to encourage the development of invention and individuality in designs for future work.

2

QUILTING DESIGNS

TECHNICALLY speaking, the term "quilting" denotes runnings of stitchings made in any materials threefold in thickness; the outer and right side textile, the center padding, of soft wool or flannel, and the under material or lining. These runnings are most commonly made in diagonal lines, crossing each other so as to form squares, diamonds, or octagonal shapes; at the same time answering the purpose of holding securely together the three materials. On Plate I, Fig. 1, notice the diagonal line arrangement, which may be quilted as shown or as in Plate IX, where it is used on the lower half of the Faith Trumbull skirt to serve as a background for the rich ornamental floral design; the lines all running one way are simple and pleasing to the eye and do not conflict in any way with the elaborate curves of the trailing vines. Fig. 2 of Plate I illustrates the crossing of lines in such a way as to form the Hanging Diamond; Fig 3 the

No. I No. II No. III

No. IV No. V No. VI PLATE I

plain Square Diamond. By grouping lines as in Fig IV,
Plate I, we have the Plaid, and as Fig. V the Broken Plaid.
Another interesting and simple design on Plate I is Fig. VI,
The Shell. This is perhaps as old as the straight line type,
yet its curves render it more difficult to quilt and less adapt-
able to combinations with floral or feather ornamental motifs.

In ancient times the diamond-shaped checks produced in
quilting, and which are now listed as background patterns,
were called "gamboised," from the word "gambeson," of Ger-
man origin. The gambeson was a medieval garment of cloth or
leather, stuffed and quilted. This was worn underneath the
habergeon or coat of mail to prevent bruises, but later it
formed the principal defensive garment.

The six diagrams shown in Plate I may be classed as the
best known gamboised or background types, which are less
numerous than the more ornamental styles of quilting almost
always combined with them.

Although ornamental quilting has been practiced in America for ages, yet the first thought of the Colonial quilter has
seemed more toward a feeling of simple beauty of line and
form than of minuteness which distinguishes the work of
the English, Asiatic, or Oriental countries, where the designs
of quilting depict nearly everything, including scenes of the
chase, battles, and ships in full sail.

Perhaps the one ornamental motif most familiar to us in
America and especially adaptable to quilting is the Ostrich
Feather or Plume. It has always furnished inexhausible
ideas for motif design and bandings. The long slender center
rib, bordered by segments of fronds, lends grace and beauty
to mass arrangement or bandings. (Notice Plate VIII and X.)
Variations of the feather have been used in wreath, scroll,
band, wave, and medallions, large and small. Aside from its
slender beauty, it offers less constructive difficulty than does
the floral motif. After marking out the center rib it is a simple matter to draw in the segments of fronds which make up
the body of the plume. The feather has ever been given
preference because it combines harmoniously with the patterns of patch or applique without losing sight of constructive
strength of line or form of the quilt, filling in substantially
the open undecorated spaces.

Plate II depicts an arrangement of feather in motifs and banding. One may easily see how the graceful curves of the plume may conform to any unusual shape to be decorated.

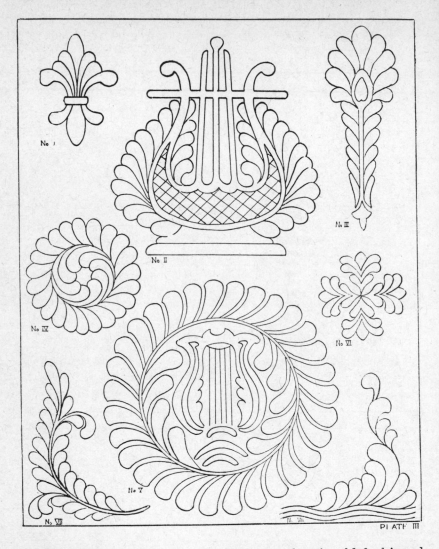

Plate III shows variations of the feather in old-fashioned quilting designs, Figs. II and V having been taken from old Colonial quilts. The use of the feather lends soft decorative tone to the more severe lines of the lyre.

Plate IV is a more modern variation of the feather in a medallion and two differently styled corners. You will notice that the border, corners, and medallion have all been constructed by the repetition of a single segment of feather.

PLATE V.

Plate V is a design of grapes and birds. This was used in the quilting of an antique bed cover, the pattern of patch which it adorned having been so nondescript as to be truly inartistic, but enriched to the extent of a museum piece by the gorgeous stitchery used in the quilting of the plain blocks and borders. The birds formed a portion of the corner design.

Plate VI. Drawings of geometric borders. Fig. I—Acanthus. Fig. II—Interlaced Diamonds. Fig. III—Woven Squares. Fig. IV—Braided Rope. Fig. V—Shell. Fig. VI—Twisted Rope.

A very beautiful piece of stuffed quilting; a white cotton bureau cover. Courtesy of Wadsworth Atheneum.

Plate VII—This is a very beautiful piece of stuffed quilting in grapes and flowers; a bureau cover. It is very typical of the style which characterizes the early American stuffed needlework. Notice how beautifully the feather design about the edge forms a frame for the graceful trailing vines and the basket of flowers within the center.

An English quilted spread, showing varied use of the ostrich feather in combination with two types of diamond background. Courtesy of Victoria Albert Museum.

Plate VIII—An English quilted spread, showing an arrangement of feather decoration in combination with two types of diamond background.

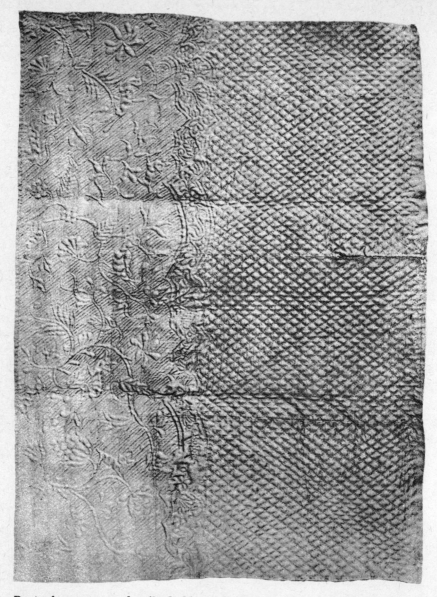

Part of a green wool quilted skirt, belonging to Faith Trumbull, wife of Daniel Wadsworth, and now in the collection of the Wadsworth Atheneum. Note the two types of background: the diamond and the diagonal line. The use of animals, birds, and trailing floral decoration shows a strong Italian influence.

Plate IX—This represents part of a green wool skirt, once the property of Faith Trumbull, wife of Daniel Wadsworth. The upper portion is quilted simply, but it represents a splendid example of gamboised style, while the bottom portion is greatly enriched by the heavy designs of trailing vines, flowers, and small animals, on a well chosen background of diagonal line quilting. Although this is an American piece of needlework the decorative detail shows a decided Italian feeling in the ornamental quilting.

Colonial stuffed and quilted bed curtain, showing the combination of birds, plumes, and floral design. Courtesy of Wadsworth Atheneum.

Plate X—This fine old bed curtain of quilted linen, though greatly worn, may still be considered an expression of the skilled Colonial quilter, both as needlewoman and as a designer. Each delicate flower and slender tendril growing out of the vase, each feather frond and little bird, are brought into relief by stuffing carefully with cotton.

*Old English yellow satin quilted dress, employing the use not only of
many floral shapes but numerous types of unusual background quilting.
Courtesy of Victoria Albert Museum.*

Plate XI—This old English dress is quilted solidly with all-over design, to which style there is a decided Chinese influence. One need hardly examine it closely to feel that it may have been an exact copy of an antique Chinese embroidery design. The scroll of the bat motif and the delicately veined foliage, in combination with the geometric background, reminds one of the Far East and of Chinese gardens and trellises. However foreign the work may be, we may see in the background stitching traces of the plaid, broken plaid, and the diamond, all of which are well known to us. This leads one to feel that these straight line patterns have come down to us from farther back than our English ancestors.

Antique Sicilian quilt made about 1400, depicting scenes from the life of Tristan. Material of buff-colored linen, with stuffed motifs, outlined in brown stitching. Courtesy of Victoria Albert Museum.

Plate XII—The date of this antique Sicilian quilt is about 1400. It is of buff-colored linen, and depicts scenes from the life of Tristan. The multitudinous figures and floral detail stitched into it are brought into relief by stuffing with wool. The tooled effect produced in the groundwork is made possible by stitching solidly and irregularly the background; this at the same time producing a flatness to the surface so that the figures appear to stand out even more. This method of background quilting was well known to our best Colonial quilters, and in constant use during the early days. At the present time it is almost never used, because of the required length of time, energy, and skill it necessitates in the execution, together with the extra expense.

Detail of Old English yellow satin quilted dress. This example shows a very decided Chinese influence in the style of its quilting. Courtesy of Victoria Albert Museum.

Plate XIII—Detail of Plate XI. Old English quilted dress. Yellow satin.

BIBLIOGRAPHY

Alexander, Vera C., *The Patchwork and Applique*

Earl, Alice Morse, *Home Life in Colonial Days* and *Customs and Fashions in Old New England*

Finley, Ruth, *Old Patchwork Quilts and the Women Who Made Them*

Hall, Eliza Calvert, *Aunt Jane of Kentucky*

McKim, Ruby Short, *One Hundred and One Patchwork Patterns*

Sexton, Carlie, *Yesterday's Quilts in Homes of Today*

Stowe, Harriet Beecher, *The Minister's Wooing*

Webster, Marie D., *Quilts, Their Story and How to Make Them*

Wheeler, Candace, *The Development of Embroidery in America*

INDEX

PART I

PART II

PART III